P9-AOI-716

Joan Didion

Revised Edition

Twayne's United States Authors Series

Warren French, Editor

University of Wales, Swansea

TUSAS 370

JOAN DIDION
Photograph courtesy of Mary Lloyd Estrin

Joan Didion

Revised Edition

By Mark Royden Winchell

Clemson University

Twayne Publishers
A Division of G. K. Hall & Co. • *Boston*

Joan Didion, Revised Edition
Mark Royden Winchell

Copyright 1989 by G. K. Hall & Co.
All rights reserved.
Published by Twayne Publishers
A Division of G. K. Hall & Co.
70 Lincoln Street
Boston, Massachusetts 02111

First edition copyright 1980, G.K. Hall & Co.
Copyediting by Barbara Sutton
Book production by John Amburg
Book design by Barbara Anderson

Typeset in 11 pt. Garamond
by Huron Valley Graphics, Inc., Ann Arbor, Michigan

Printed on permanent/durable acid-free paper
and bound in the United States of America

Library of Congress Cataloging-in-Publication Data

Winchell, Mark Royden, 1948–
    Joan Didion / by Mark Royden Winchell.—Rev. ed.
        p.   cm.—(Twayne's United States authors series ; TUSAS 370)
    Bibliography: p.
    Includes index.
    ISBN 0-8057-7535-8 (alk. paper)
    1. Didion, Joan—Criticism and interpretation. I. Title.
II. Series.
PS3554.I33Z95 1989
813'.54—dc19   88-37950
                                                                              CIP

For my wife, Donna

Contents

About the Author

Mark Royden Winchell has published books on William F. Buckley, Jr., and Leslie Fiedler in Twayne's United States Authors Series and monographs on Horace McCoy and John Gregory Dunne in the Boise State University Western Writers Series. Over the past decade his work has appeared in the *American Spectator,* the *Mississippi Quarterly, Chronicles of Culture, The History of Southern Literature,* and numerous other publications. In addition, he is a frequent contributor to the *Sewanee Review,* the *Canadian Review of American Studies,* and the book section of the *Atlanta Journal-Constitution.* His most recent book, *Talmadge: A Political Legacy, A Politician's Life* (written in collaboration with Herman E. Talmadge), was published by Peachtree Publishers, Ltd., of Atlanta in 1987. He has also edited a collection of essays on Vanderbilt writers, which will be published by the Louisiana State University Press in the near future, and a special country music issue of the *Southern Quarterly.* Future projects include a Western Writers Series monograph on William Humphrey and a Twayne Series study of three neoconservative critics. Winchell received his Ph.D. from Vanderbilt University in 1978. He is currently professor of English at Clemson University, where he lives with his wife, composition scholar Donna Haisty Winchell, and a stuffed bear named Lazarus.

Preface

Since the first version of this study appeared in 1980, Joan Didion has begun to receive the scholarly attention that befits an important contemporary writer. In addition to a growing body of articles in critical journals, she has been the focus of one other book-length study and an uneven collection of "essays and conversations." Thus, Didion has clearly found her niche among those writers who are taught, discussed, and generally taken seriously in academic circles. Whatever other virtues or defects my own book may have possessed, it seems to have been on-target in judging Didion's work worthy of extended comment. But why come back with a second edition less than a decade later?

The first, and easiest, answer to that question is that Didion has produced some more work—three books and a handful of interesting uncollected magazine pieces—that need to be looked at. Besides, any study of an active contemporary writer is likely to become obsolete faster than a late-model automobile. Ever since it became legitimate to write about the work of living authors, criticism has itself been more a disposable commodity than a judgment for the ages. So, it is high time to check back in on Joan Didion to see what she has done since last we left her.

But even if that were not the case, I would appreciate the opportunity to improve upon my earlier efforts. Benjamin Franklin once noted that the main difference between books and life is that with books you sometimes have the opportunity to do a revised edition. I have yet to write anything that could not profit from revision, and the original version of this book is no exception. The function of the critic, according to T.S. Eliot, is to correct taste. Occasionally, it is the critic's own taste that is in need of correction.

The first six chapters of this book deal exclusively with Didion's nonfiction. Rather than treating her two collections—*Slouching Towards Bethlehem* (1968) and *The White Album* (1979)—separately, I have organized my discussion thematically. Chapter 1 is biographical; chapter 2 focuses on Didion's views on literature, the arts, and morality; chapter 3 on social classes and lifestyles; chapter 4 on politics; chapter 5 on people; and chapter 6 on selected places. Chapter 7, which deals with Didion's writings about California, concludes with an analysis of her first novel, *Run River* (1963).

We look at Didion's short fiction in chapter 8, her writings about Hollywood—including her Hollywood novel *Play It as It Lays* (1970)—in chapter 9, and her Central American novel—*A Book of Common Prayer* (1977)—in chapter 10. That leads us to a discussion of her two recent nonfiction books about Central America, *Salvador* (1983) and *Miami* (1987), in chapter 11. Chapter 12 is concerned with Didion's writings about our western-most frontier of Hawaii, particularly her Hawaiian novel, *Democracy* (1984). Chapter 13 serves as a conclusion, if not to Joan Didion's career or to criticism of that career, at least to this particular phase of the on-going dialogue.

Mark Royden Winchell

Clemson University

Acknowledgments

Among the many individuals who helped make this book possible, three deserve particular mention. First, there is Joan Didion, who wrote the books and allowed me to quote from them. Next, there is Warren French, who had the prescience to believe that Didion was worthy of a place in the Twayne series, the generosity to believe that a novice critic could do the job, and the discernment to realize when the job needed to be done again. Finally, there is my wife, Donna, who lets me use her computer, corrects my errors, indulges my idiosyncracies, and displays a tolerance in comparison to which Chaucer's Griselda seems a mean-spirited shrew.

Chronology

1934	Joan Didion born in Sacramento, California, 5 December.
1952	Graduates from C. K. McClatchy High School in Sacramento.
1953	Enters the University of California at Berkeley in February.
1956	Graduates from Berkeley; publishes first story— "Sunset"—in student literary magazine *Occident;* wins *Vogue*'s "Prix de Paris" award.
1956–1964	Lives in New York; writes for *Vogue, Mademoiselle,* and *National Review.*
1963	*Run River.*
1964	Marries John Gregory Dunne in January; moves back to California in June; short story "Coming Home" (*Saturday Evening Post*).
1964–1966	Writes regular movie column for *Vogue;* publishes essays in *Holiday, Saturday Evening Post, New York Times Magazine,* and *American Scholar.*
1965	Short story "The Welfare Island Ferry" (*Harper's Bazaar*).
1966	Adopts infant daughter Quintana.
1967	Short story "When Did Music Come This Way? Children Dear, Was It Yesterday?" (*Denver Quarterly*).
1967–1969	With Dunne shares "Points West" column in *Saturday Evening Post.*
1968	*Slouching Towards Bethlehem.*
1969–1970	Writes column for *Life.*
1970	*Play It as It Lays.*
1971	*The Panic in Needle Park* (film).
1972	Film version of *Play It as It Lays.*
1972–1979	Publishes in *New York Times Book Review, New York Review of Books,* and *Esquire.*

1975   Serves as Regents lecturer, University of California at Berkeley.

1976–1977   With Dunne shares "The Coast" column in *Esquire*.

1976   *A Star Is Born* (film).

1977   *A Book of Common Prayer*.

1978   *Telling Stories*.

1979   *The White Album*.

1979–1980   With Dunne shares column in *New West*.

1979–1987   Publishes in *New York Review of Books* and *Michigan Quarterly Review*.

1981   Film version of *True Confessions*.

1982   Visits El Salvador

1983   *Salvador*.

1984   *Democracy*.

1987   *Miami*.

Chapter One

How Many Miles to Babylon?

Joan Didion has been called everything from a "fantastically brilliant writer" to an "entrepreneur of anxiety."[1] Her admirers have compared her to T. S. Eliot and Nathanael West. And yet neoconservative critic Joseph Epstein has dismissed her as a purveyor of "freeway existentialism," and one disgruntled feminist has characterized her as "a curious creature, whose sense of literature and life is common, disappointingly conventional, and always problematical."[2] No less an authority than James Dickey has called her "the finest woman prose stylist writing in English today."[3]

The woman thus described is, at five-feet-two and ninety-one pounds, an unimposing figure who dislikes public appearances. She speaks in a nervous voice that is frequently inaudible and accounts for her success as a reporter by saying, "I am so physically small, so temperamentally unobtrusive, and so neurotically inarticulate that people tend to forget that my presence runs counter to their best interests."[4] Despite heavy medication, she spends between three and five days a month in bed with a migraine headache and suffers from a form of multiple sclerosis. In the late sixties, she was diagnosed as "a *personality in process of deterioration with abundant signs of failing defenses and increasing inability of the ego to mediate the world of reality and to cope with normal stress.*"[5] She is also a wife and mother, a successful screenwriter, a member of the prestigious American Institute of Arts and Letters, and a fifth-generation Californian who, at the age of eighteen, wanted simultaneously to be both a medieval scholar and a Rose Bowl princess.

In reading Joan Didion's nonfiction (and parts of her novels as well), it is tempting to ignore the critical dictum that one should trust the tale and not the teller, for with Didion the two frequently overlap. Her writing seems to be a search for identity, an attempt to create a fictive persona with which to impose artistic coherence upon the randomness of life. What she strives for in the written word is what most of us strive for in a somewhat less deliberate and less verbal form—self-knowledge.

In her frequently anthologized essay "On Keeping a Notebook" Didion even goes so far as to suggest that self-knowledge has more to do with imagination than with memory. For example, "the cracked crab that I recall having for lunch the day my father came home from Detroit in 1945 must certainly be embroidery, worked into the day's pattern to lend verisimilitude," but it is that cracked crab that, years later, makes the whole afternoon come alive for her. The same is true of a childhood August that Didion spent in Vermont: "[P]erhaps there never were flurries in the night wind," she admits; "and maybe no one else felt the ground hardening and the summer already dead even as we pretended to bask in it, but that was how it felt to me, and it might as well have snowed, could have snowed, did snow" (*STB* 134). Didion's writing is filled with aesthetic equivalents of cracked crab and August snow. And if they tell us less than we might like to know about the factual details of her life, they tell us all we need to know about our reason for being interested in that life. It is for the sake of the tale that we pursue the teller.

Notes on the Native Daughter

Joan Didion was born in Sacramento, California, in December 1934, the daughter of Frank Reese and Eduene Jerrett Didion. As Katherine Usher Henderson points out, however, neither Didion's parents nor her younger brother Jimmy plays a very prominent role in her autobiographical writing.[6] Of much greater importance is the Northern California setting itself. Didion's great-great-great grandmother Nancy Hardin Cornwall came west on a wagon train in 1846, traveling most of the way with the Donner-Reed Party, only to cut north to Oregon before her companions made their way into history by eating their dead. Didion seems to carry the heritage of the frontier in her genes and with it a sense of life's very contingency.

Young Joan's California childhood was itself interrupted by the contingency of history when, two days after her seventh birthday, the Japanese attacked Pearl Harbor. This event, she recalls, "meant war and my father going away and makeshift Christmases in rented rooms near Air Corps bases and nothing the same ever again" (*STB* 189). But with the end of war came a return to Sacramento and an adolescence that coincided with the expansive optimism of America in the late forties. The author recalls with particular vividness the summers of those years when she would go with her mother and brother to "a place on the Marin County coast called Stinson Beach." Although Didion does not flinch at describing the tawdriness of this locale (it was "unkempt, desolate, so rickety that geraniums obscured even the sunbleached Coca-Cola signs"), there is also an elegiac fondness in her memories of "playing 'Ghost Riders in the Sky' on the jukebox in the combination grocery store, drugstore, and Greyhound bus station." The social high spot of her eleventh summer was "a day's excursion to San Francisco to have my chest X-rayed."[7]

By the time she was fourteen, Didion was popular enough to be inducted into the Mañana Club, a sorority at Sacramento's C. K. McClatchy High School. Her initiation took place at the California Governor's Mansion, home of fellow member Nina Warren, who was daughter of the state's chief executive. (For Didion that old house, a Victorian Gothic mansion that has since been replaced by a modern ranch house built by Ronald Reagan, represents the old California of her childhood before real estate developers and aerospace engineers had transformed the region into an extension of the Sunbelt.) During the initiation, she was blindfolded as the other girls hurled mild insults at her. When Nina Warren told Didion that she was "stuck on herself," she "learned for the first time that my face to the world was not necessarily the face in my mirror" (*WA* 71).

An even more severe adolescent trauma occurred when, as a senior in high school, Didion received a letter rejecting her application for admission to Stanford. The mimeographed letter informing her of her fate began "Dear Joan"—although the writer had never met her—and was signed by an admissions nerd named Rixford K. Snyder. After the initial shock, Didion's humiliation became complete when she realized that all of her friends who had applied to Stanford had been accepted. Since the only appropriate response was suicide, she sat on the edge of the bathtub trying to summon up the courage to swallow an old bottle of codeine and Empirim. "I saw myself in an oxygen tent," she recalls, "with Rixford K. Snyder hovering outside, although how the news was to reach Rixford K. Snyder was a plot point that troubled me even as I counted out the tablets."

Instead of taking the pills, she spent the rest of the spring in the sort of "sullen but mild rebellion" characteristic of the American fifties—"sitting around drive-ins, listening to Tulsa evangelists on the car radio." That summer she fell in love with an aspiring golf pro and "spent a lot of time watching him practice putting."[8] Her rebellion worn out, she enrolled that fall for a couple of hours a day in a junior college to make up the credits she needed for admission to the University of California at Berkeley.

The Artist as a Young Woman

When Joan Didion returned to Berkeley as a Regents' Lecturer in 1975, nearly twenty years after her own graduation, she found herself regressing aimlessly into "the ghetto life of the student" she had lived in the fifties. She found herself eating tacos for dinner, smoking too many cigarettes, and wearing a shapeless blue blazer and no makeup. It seemed to her that in the two decades since she had left campus nothing had changed:

There, just a block or two off the campus—the campus with its 5,000 courses, its 4 million books, its 5 million manuscripts, the campus with its cool glades and clear creeks and lucid views—lay this mean wasteland of small venture capital, this unweeded garden in which everything cost more than it was worth. Coffee on Telegraph Avenue was served neither hot nor cold. Food was slopped lukewarm onto chipped plates. Pita bread was stale, curries were rank, tatty "Indian" stores offered faded posters and shoddy silks. Bookstores featured sections on the occult. Drug buys were in progress up and down the street.[9]

If anything, what Didion was witnessing was more a case of relapse than of stagnation. The Berkeley she knew in the fifties and seventies was a far cry from the legendary campus of the intervening decade. A national metonymy for student radicalism, Berkeley in the sixties was the home of Mario Savio and the free speech movement and later of Vietnam Day protests against the American war in Indochina. To Didion's generation, however, that would have seemed like pretty jejune stuff. Hers was the silent generation, she tells us, "neither, as some thought, because we shared the period's official optimism nor, as others thought, because we feared its official repression" (WA 206). Instead, she would have us believe that it was superior sophistication and philosophical cynicism that kept her and her classmates off the barricades. Whether or not such a generalization can be applied to an entire generation, it is clear that this is how Didion recalls her own undergraduate years.

When she remembers Berkeley, one of her most vivid recollections is of lying on a leather couch in a fraternity house and reading a book by Lionel Trilling while a middle-aged man tried vainly to pick out the melodic line to "Blue Room" on a piano. "I can hear and see it still," she writes, "the wrong note in 'We will thrive on / Keep alive on,' the sunlight falling through the big windows, the man picking up his drink and beginning again and telling me, without ever saying a word, something I had not known before about bad marriages and wasted time and looking backward" (*WA* 205). Other memories are of "a woman picking daffodils in the rain one day when I was walking in the hills," of "a teacher who drank too much one night and revealed his fright and bitterness," and of "my real joy at discovering for the first time how language worked, at discovering, for example, that the central line of *Heart of Darkness* was a postscript" (*WA* 207).

Although Didion did not learn how to write at Berkeley (that would come later during her days at *Vogue*), her experience in Mark Schorer's creative writing class did cement her commitment to writing as a vocation. She remembers being a naive and inexperienced country girl in a class full of older, more experienced, and more exotic students. Not only did her classmates seem to have lived more interesting lives, but also to have more of the raw material for the five short stories required in the course. Didion attended every meeting of the class, heard other people's stories read aloud, and never spoke. When she ransacked her closet for clothes that would make her invisible, she came up only with a dirty raincoat. Because of a kind of adolescent paralysis and a fear of not being good enough, she produced only three of the required five stories and came away with a course grade of B solely as a result of what she calls Schorer's "infinite kindness to and acuity about his students."[10]

Having endured that rite of passage, Didion spent her junior and senior years living alone in a large bare apartment, where she read Camus, Orwell, and Henry James. (She had lived her first two years at Berkeley in the Tri Delt House, but had moved out not over any issue, but because she disliked living with sixty other people.) She also "watched a flowering plum come in and out of blossom, and at night, most nights, . . . walked outside and looked up to where the cyclotron and the bevatron glowed on the dark hillside, unspeakable mysteries which engaged me, in the style of my time, only personally" (*WA* 207–8). Summing up her later experience, she writes, "I got out of Berkeley and went to New York and came to Los Angeles. What I have made for myself is personal, but is not exactly peace" (*WA* 208).

In 1956 Didion graduated from Berkeley and won *Vogue's* "Prix de Paris" contest and, with it, a job on the magazine. She lived for the next eight years in New York writing for *National Review* and *Mademoiselle,* as well as for *Vogue* itself. Also during those years she appeared for three consecutive nights on a television quiz show called "Crosswits"; published her first novel, *Run River;* and married a young writer for *Time* magazine, John Gregory Dunne. However, none of this is mentioned in "Goodbye to All That," Didion's definitive essay on her years in New York. Instead, she dredges her emotional memory to convey something of the mood of her relationship with the enchanted city of the East.

Much has been written about the significance of the journey west in American life and literature. The lure of the frontier with its promise of freedom and a new start is an essential American myth. But there is also the dream of the East, which exerts an equally powerful if very different sort of imaginative appeal. For someone of Didion's small-town western background, Manhattan must have seemed the very pinnacle of civilization. She says that she loved New York "the way you love the first person who ever touches you and never love anyone quite that way again" (*STB* 228). Indeed, one suspects that the city was for her what Daisy Buchanan was for Jay Gatsby. "New York was no mere city," she writes. "It was instead an infinitely romantic notion, the mysterious nexus of all love and money and power, the shining and perishable dream itself. To think of 'living' there was to reduce the miraculous to the mundane; one does not 'live' at Xanadu" (*STB* 231).

Didion prefaces her essay with a nursery rhyme, which serves as a highly suggestive epigraph. It reads:

> How many miles to Babylon?
> Three score miles and ten—
> Can I get there by candlelight?
> Yes, and back again—
> If your feet are nimble and light
> You can get there by candlelight.

In commenting on this rhyme Iona and Peter Opie point out that two interpretations are most frequently advanced for the term "Babylon." One holds that the term is actually a corruption of "Babyland," while the more accepted view sees Babylon as "the far-away luxurious city of seventeenth-century usage."[11] In a sense both interpretations work here. For Didion New York was at once a "far-away luxurious city" and a town "for only the very young" (*STB* 227)—until finally becoming a place of unbearable exile. Early on in the essay she writes, "Part of what I want to tell you is what it is like to be young in New York, how six months can become eight years with the deceptive ease of a film dissolve, for that is how those years appear to me now, in a long sequence of sentimental dissolves and old-fashioned trick shots— the Seagram Building fountains dissolve into snowflakes, I enter a revolving door at twenty and come out a good deal older, and on a different street" (*STB* 227).

"Goodbye to All That" (the title apparently borrowed from Robert Graves's autobiography) is divided into four sections, indicated by double-line breaks, which correspond to different stages in the author's relationship with New York. At first, she is the ingenuous young Sacramento girl who spent her first three days in the big city wrapped in blankets in a hotel room air-conditioned to 35 degrees as she "tried to get over a bad cold and a high fever" (*STB* 226). She didn't call a doctor because she knew no doctors; she didn't call anyone to turn down the air conditioner because she didn't know how much to tip whoever might come. "Was anyone ever so young?" she asks. "I am here to tell you that someone was" (*STB* 227). According to Didion, youth is not just a time of life but a state of delusion—a delusion that the emotional costs we incur in life need never be paid or can be indefinitely deferred. When those costs began coming due for her, her youth was over. And so too was the enchantment of Babylon.

The process of disillusionment came only gradually to Didion. During her early years in New York, she was still able to give glib advice to a depressed friend, never realizing that she would eventually suffer his fate. Throughout the second section of her essay (after the initial naivete had worn off), we see Didion living in New York as if she had been transported to a magic kingdom. In the third section she is simply *living* there—staying up all night (the hint of insomnia is telling), going to work on two or three hours' sleep, moving from one meagerly furnished apartment to another, and breaking ties with friends. By the fourth section she seems on the verge of a nervous breakdown, disabused of her youthful fantasies and unable to function in the workaday world. Fortunately, she marries a kindly man who does not insist on her cooking supper and who eventually moves with her back to California.

"Goodbye to All That" has a structure that is neither thematic nor chronological so much as impressionistic. (The author's double focus is

continually emphasized by such phrases as "I remember" and "In retro-
spect it seemed to me.") Didion's memory is replete with the names of
places, but other people are almost never named. (We know that her
husband used to take her to Michael's Pub and to Toots Shor's for
dinner; but we don't know who her husband is, how she met him, or
much about their life together.) When other people do appear it is in
vague, generic terms: we read of "a friend who complained of having
been around too long" (STB 227–28), of "someone who did have the
West Village number" (STB 235), of people who "had moved to Dallas
or had gone on Antabuse or had bought a farm in New Hampshire"
(STB 238). No, real people don't live in Xanadu, Didion seems to be
saying. But some come to painful maturity just passing through.

The Ties That Bind

Joan Didion and John Gregory Dunne were married in January
1964, and that June they moved to California for a temporary visit that
has lasted ever since. Despite a lean first year in which they made
$7,000 between them, Didion and Dunne began to establish them-
selves as accomplished free-lance journalists and bought successive
homes with their earnings from screenwriting. Their film credits include *The Panic in Needle Park* (1971), the 1976 remake of *A Star Is
Born* (starring Barbra Streisand), on which they made a small fortune
although they left the picture before it was completed, and film versions of her *Play It as It Lays* (1972) and his *True Confessions* (1981).

The Dunnes have always enjoyed a close working relationship, editing
each other's prose and sharing a series of magazine columns over the years
(first with the *Saturday Evening Post* from June 1966 to January 1969,
then with *Esquire* from February 1976 to December 1977, and finally
with *New West* from late 1979 to mid-1980). In 1982 Dunne reckoned
that their marriage had consisted of "15 years of good days and three years
of bad days, . . . a terrific ratio."[12] If their readers are surprised by the
relative stability of that marriage, it is because the two authors have not
hesitated to write about the bad moments. As Dunne puts it, "Life is
difficult enough without having to try to find material."[13]

In addition to the normal pressures of married life, the Dunnes had
to contend for years with a situation in which the wife was more
prominent than the husband. Didion's collection of essays *Slouching
Towards Bethlehem* (1968) and her novels *Play It as It Lays* (1972) and *A
Book of Common Prayer* (1977) achieved considerable critical and popular

success, while Dunne's three nonfiction books—*Delano* (1967), *The Studio* (1969), and *Vegas: A Memoir of a Dark Season* (1974)—received much less notice in the nation's major book reviews. That situation changed dramatically when Dunne discovered the rich literary possibilities of depicting Irish-American culture in the trauma of assimilation, something he has called the "mother lode" of his muse. Thus far, he has mined that mother lode for three vastly entertaining and intermittently profound novels—*True Confessions* (1978), *Dutch Shea, Jr.* (1982), and *The Red, White and Blue* (1987). As a result, he is no longer known in literary circles as "Mr. Joan Didion."

Even when things were not going smoothly in their personal lives, Didion and Dunne continued to work well together (a sort of literary Sonny and Cher). When Dunne made a neurotic hegira to Las Vegas, he would call home to share notes with Didion, who characteristically helped him edit the book he produced from the experience. He tells us in that book that on one such occasion Joan told him she was lonely and depressed and that the septic tank had overflowed:

There was a crash pad next door and one of the couples had taken to boffing on the grass in clear view of our daughter's bedroom window. . . . The maid had quit, the fire insurance had been canceled and the engine in the Corvette had seized on the Ventura Freeway. The Chevrolet agency refused to honor the warranty on the Corvette and so she had called Detroit and told the head of public relations at General Motors that if the warranty was not honored she was going to drive the car to Detroit and burn the motherfucker on the lawn of John Z. DeLorean, vice-president and general manager of the Chevrolet division of General Motors. The head of public relations had suggested she see a psychiatrist. "What's new with you?" she said.[14]

A third member was added to the Dunne family in 1966, when John and Joan adopted an infant daughter they named Quintana Roo. (In 1978 Dunne even published a collection of essays entitled *Quintana & Friends*.) In her essay "On Going Home," Didion writes about returning to Sacramento for Quintana's first birthday. Her primary concern, however, is with her own lost past not her daughter's uncertain future. For Didion home is a temporal as well as a spatial concept (which is why so many of us share Thomas Wolfe's inability to go there again). When the children of Didion's generation left home, it was a rite of passage she suspects is totally irrelevant to the children of Quintana's generation. She recalls a few weeks earlier having seen a young girl on drugs dance for the cash prize in an amateur topless contest in a bar in San Francisco. "There was no particular sense of moment about this," she recalls, "none of the effect of romantic degradation, of 'dark journey,' for which my generation strived so assiduously. What sense could that girl possibly make of, say, *Long Day's Journey into Night?*" (*STB* 166).

Didion would like to pass on to her daughter the various traditions she associates with the stable agrarian life of her childhood, but she realizes that she cannot even recover those traditions for herself except through memory (perhaps embroidered somewhat by cracked crab and August snow). Quintana, like the girl in the amateur topless contest, was "born of the fragmentation after World War II" (*STB* 165). Unable to give her an italicized sense of *home* for her birthday, Didion can only "give her a xylophone and a sundress from Madeira, and promise to tell her a funny story" (*STB* 168).

Unfortunately, it would be wrong to assume that because Didion's present life is different from the one she knew as a child that she has succeeded in finding a new kind of "home." On the contrary, she depicts herself as presently a lost soul cast adrift in the modern world. The title and tone of her December 1969 *Life* column, "A Problem of Making Connections," is characteristic of most of her autobiographical writing. This essay is direct and immediate: Didion addresses the reader as "you" and uses the present tense. She tells us that she is at the Royal Hawaiian Hotel in Honolulu with her husband and daughter during a time of personal crisis, involving some unspecified marital stress. We see the family sitting in their room waiting for news of a possible tidal wave: "The bulletin, when it comes, is a distinct anticlimax: Midway reports no unusual wave action. My husband switches off the TV set and stares out the window. I avoid his eyes and brush the baby's hair. In the absence of a natural disaster we are left again to our own uneasy devices. We are here on this island in the middle of the Pacific in lieu of filing for divorce."[15] Not surprisingly, John Gregory Dunne helped his wife revise and proofread this piece as they drove to the post office to mail it to the mainland.

Like so many professional women, Didion has not always had an easy time reconciling the demands of her career with the role of conventional mother and homemaker. The resulting tension and guilt are the subject of another December 1969 *Life* column entitled "In Praise of Unhung Wreaths and Love." Didion begins this sketch by telling us of the idyllic sort of Christmas she had planned on having, of the house filled with candles and star jasmine, of the things she and her daughter would do together. ("We would make pomegranate jelly and wrap the jars in red cellophane. We would sit at the piano and pick out carols together.") In fact, she is not home to do any of these things, but is in New York with her husband to write a movie about heroin users. She is typing her column "in a deserted office where the only suggestion of human life is the faint clatter of an untended AP wire." The next day she and Dunne are scheduled to interview a heroin dealer "in a Blimpy Burger on a desolate West Side street." Their contact promises to "be there around noon. . . . Or anyway between noon and four."

Making pomegranate jelly and hanging wreaths are the sort of Christmas traditions Didion associates with her italicized sense of home. But the message that runs through her writing is that that sort of home exists only as the subject of elegy. She is where she is in that pre-Christmas season not by accident, but because that is where she wants to be—or more precisely because that is where what she wants to do requires her to be. And besides, it is a hopelessly romantic (and for Didion self-lacerating) notion that "three-year-olds and their mothers need to make pomegranate jelly together to learn about family love." "The baby will know something about family love on Christmas," she concludes, "because she knows something about it today, and she will also know something about its complexities."[16]

Woman of the Year

In 1979 Joan Didion published a selection of her essays from the 1970s and the late 60s under the title *The White Album*. While appearing occasionally in the *New York Times Book Review* and the *New York Review of Books*, she has not had a regular deadline since then (except for the six months or so she and Dunne wrote for *New West*). Thus freed to work on more substantial projects, she has produced two full-length nonfiction books—*Salvador* (1983) and *Miami* (1987)—and a fourth novel, *Democracy* (1984). As a result of these and earlier accomplishments she has appeared on enough talk shows and been featured in enough national magazines to become a minor celebrity. Although she seems highly uncomfortable in this role, her status as a media figure did provide the basis for an amusing *White Album* essay entitled "On the Road."

From this essay, describing the promotional tour Didion made on behalf of *A Book of Common Prayer*, we derive a sense of the frenetic pace of life lived from airport to airport. She tells us that she "began to see America as my own, a child's map over which my child and I could skim and light at will. We spoke not of cities but of airports. If rain fell at Logan we could find sun at Dulles. Bags lost at O'Hare could be found at Dallas/Fort Worth" (WA 176). When she landed it was to give press interviews and appear on a seemingly endless series of local talk shows, all of which asked the same question—"Where are we heading?" "The set for this discussion," Didion recalls, "was always the same: a cozy oasis of wicker and ferns in the wilderness of cables and cameras and Styrofoam coffee cups that was the actual studio. On wicker settees across the nation I expressed my conviction that we were heading 'into an era' of whatever the clock seemed to demand" (WA 175).

If a large number of Didion's writings evoke memorable visual images, this one relies primarily on the author's ear for a particular kind of American speech. As she makes her rounds on the opinion circuit, certain trendy ideas and catch phrases get jumbled in surrealistic profusion. She "listened attentively . . . to people who seemed convinced that the 'texture' of their lives had been agreeably or adversely affected by conversion to the politics of joy, by regression to lapidary bleakness, by the Sixties, by the Fifties, by the recent change in administrations and by the sale of The Thorn Birds to paper for one-million-nine" (WA 178). And always there is that ubiquitous question: "Where are we heading?" "I don't know where you're heading," Didion says, "in the studio attached to the last of these antennae, my eyes fixed on still another of the neon FLEETWOOD MAC signs that flickered that spring in radio stations from coast to coast, but I'm heading home" (WA 179).

One is tempted to say that behind the celebrity is a hypersensitive woman racked by insecurity and self-doubt. But that would suggest an element of concealment that really isn't there. Few writers have been as open as Didion in discussing their personal anxieties in print. Except for occasional thrusts of self-deprecatory humor and detached analysis, she comes perilously close to being the journalistic equivalent of a confessional poet. For example, in the title essay of The White Album Didion tells us that in 1968 while she, Mrs. Ronald Reagan, the Olympic swimmer Debbie Meyer, and ten other California women were being named Los Angeles Times "Woman of the Year," she was also being treated for vertigo and nausea at the outpatient psychiatric clinic of Saint John's Hospital in Santa Monica. It is almost inconceivable that someone who exhibits such control and lucidity in her writing could be as close to the edge personally as Didion claims to have been in the late sixties and early seventies. But as Edmund Wilson in "The Wound and the Bow" and numerous other psychobiographical critics have shown, personal misfortune is often the breeding ground of literary genius.

The exquisite sensibility evident in Didion's writing is forged at least in part by a feeling of psychological vulnerability and the experience of severe physical pain. We get a glimpse into one of the main sources of that vulnerability and pain in the *White Album* essay "In Bed." In this piece Didion admits something she had tried to deny for years, that "the physiological error called migraine is . . . central to the given of my life" (*WA* 168). After years of resistance, during which she "sat through lectures in Middle English and presentations to advertisers with involuntary tears running down the right side of my face, threw up in washrooms, stumbled home by instinct, emptied ice trays into my bed and tried to freeze the pain in my right temple, wished only for a neurosurgeon who would do a lobotomy on house call, and cursed my imagination" (*WA* 169), she finally realized that migraine was something she would have to live with the way some people live with diabetes.

It is often true that someone who has known a particular deprivation experiences life more fully when that deprivation is gone. The blind man whose sight has been restored, the deaf person who can now hear, the recovering alcoholic who no longer drinks can sense things that the rest of us take for granted. Didion hints that much the same thing is true for her when her migraine is gone. "The migraine has acted as a circuit breaker," she writes, "and the fuses have emerged intact. There is a pleasant convalescent euphoria. I open the windows and feel the air, eat gratefully, sleep well. I notice the particular nature of a flower in a glass on the stair landing. I count my blessings" (*WA* 172).

Didion admits that she is the sort of personality inclined to migraine, someone the doctors describe as "ambitious, inward, intolerant of error, rather rigidly organized, perfectionist." If persons observing her hair or her house might not readily apply those adjectives to Didion, that is because they fail to realize that perfectionism can also "take the form of spending most of a week writing and rewriting and not writing a single paragraph" (*WA* 171). The fact that many knowledgeable observers believe she has perfected this art about as well as anyone now writing seems not to satisfy Didion's migraine personality, that demon within that tells her she is not yet good enough. At the height of her success she observed, "At nineteen I had wanted to write. At 40 I still wanted to write, and nothing that had happened in the years between made me any more certain that I could."[17]

Chapter Two

Style as Character

In her essay on artist Georgia O'Keeffe, Joan Didion contends that *"style is character"* (*WA* 127). This would appear to be Didion's own personal creed as she approaches questions of ethics and aesthetics. Although we can infer as much from her imaginative writing, we need not go to the trouble of doing so, because the evidence is pretty explicit in her critical observations on literature, the arts, and personal morality. Philosophically, this may be little more than a variation on the Keatsian formula, "Beauty is truth, truth beauty," but it has fairly serious implications for Didion's life as a writer. Above all, it means that her sense of taste and decorum carries with it the force of a categorical imperative. If this means that some will regard her as an elitist snob, then so be it. As she notes in her review of John Cheever's *Falconer:* "Some of us are not Jews. Neither are some of us Southerners, nor children of the Iroquois, nor the inheritors of any other notably dark and bloodied ground. Some of us are even Episcopalians."[1]

A Way of Saying *I*

From her early contributions to *National Review* through her more recent pieces in the *New York Times Book Review* and the *New York Review of Books,* John Didion has commented extensively on other writers. In going back over her critical essays and reviews, we can begin to generalize about Didion's own literary sensibility. We can say, for example, that the writers she admires tend to be expert craftsmen who also possess what Matthew Arnold called "high seriousness." For this reason, Didion refuses to excuse what she regards as the moral lapses of even the most accomplished prose stylist. (While conceding the technical virtues of Salinger's *Franny and Zooey,* for example, she takes its author to task for his "tendency to flatter the essential triviality within each of his readers."[2]) By the same token, she expresses her regard for such artists as Elizabeth Hardwick, Mary McCarthy, and Jean Stafford "because they are very good writers and because their writing reflects

15

their respective moral sensibilities."[3] "I have a very rigid sense of right and wrong," she says. "What I mean is, I use the words all the time. Even the smallest things. A table can be right or wrong. . . . In order to maintain a semblance of purposeful behavior on this earth you have to believe that things are right or wrong."[4]

Just as she has little regard for amoral stylists, so too does Didion disapprove of artless polemicists. In her review of Doris Lessing's *Briefing for a Descent into Hell,* she accuses Lessing of having written a novel entirely of ideas, "not a novel about the play of ideas in the lives of certain characters but a novel in which the characters exist only as markers in the presentation of an idea" (*WA* 120). Didion goes on to mention a slighting reference made by a character in another Lessing novel to writers who think in terms of artistic problems. This is just the sort of dichotomy between life and art that Didion refuses to admit. "*Madame Bovary* told us more about bourgeois life than several generations of Marxists have," she notes, "but there does not seem much doubt that Flaubert saw it as an artistic problem" (*WA* 122–23). "That Mrs. Lessing does not," Didion concludes, "suggests her particular dilemma" (*WA* 123).

Ultimately, then, Didion does not equate moral art with mere didacticism. Although she does not consider technical brilliance to be the sole criterion for judging fiction, she nevertheless sees such brilliance as an essential characteristic of all good writing. One might even say that for Didion a novelist's primary—though not exclusive—*moral* obligation is to be a proficient craftsman.

While her literary opinions are to be found predominantly in her reviews of specific novels, Didion offers us a more general statement of her critical attitudes in her *National Review* essay "Questions About the New Fiction." Here, she is trashing the sort of experimental writers who have abandoned a realistic narrative line for self-referential word games. Whether these writers be called neofabulists, postmodernists, metafictionists, or (in Gore Vidal's memorable phrase) purveyors of "American plastic," they have abandoned the traditional faith that literature is of central importance to life. (Tom Wolfe believes that it is for this reason that the tradition of narrative realism has been reinvigorated in our time not by novelists, but by the new journalists.)

Those writers who come in for Didion's overt or implied censure include Thomas Berger, Thomas Pynchon, J. P. Donleavy, Bruce Jay Freidman, Kurt Vonnegut, and Joseph Heller. She complains, for example, of Heller's "disinclination to go all the way with anything,

his insistence on having it both ways, all ways, any way his fancy led."
She argues that "for four hundred pages of *Catch-22*, World War II was
a fraud and the only virtue survival, while in the last few pages we
learned that the war was worth fighting but some of the officers were
maniacs, a rather different proposition."

Didion sums up the dilemma of the committed writer of fiction
quite well when she says: "Everyone wants to tell the truth, and everyone recognizes that to juxtapose even two sentences is necessarily to tell
a lie, to tell less than one knows, to distort the situation, cut off its
ambiguities and so its possibilities. To write with style is to fight lying
all the way. Nonetheless, this is what must be done or we end up
maundering. We tell nothing. To tell something, really tell it, takes a
certain kind of moral hardness."[5] Her list of those who possess this
moral hardness includes Norman Mailer,[6] John Hawkes, Bernard Mala-
mud, Flannery O'Connor, Vladimir Nabokov (sometimes), John Cheever, Katherine Anne Porter, and Saul Bellow (in *Seize the Day* but not in
Herzog).

Conceivably, Didion's opinions have changed since she wrote this
article at age thirty. Her three novels published since then are certainly
more innovative technically than her maiden effort *Run River*. In particular, the points of view in both *A Book of Common Prayer* and *Democracy* reject traditional notions of authorial reliability for the sort of
epistemological relativism often associated with the new fiction. Still,
Didion stops well short of the moral and metaphysical frivolity of the
more precious postmodernists. Her narrators may not always be certain
of the truth, but they never doubt that the truth is a matter of ultimate
significance. At her most relativistic she is closer to William Faulkner
than to John Barth.

In the revealing comments she has made about her own writing
process, Joan Didion has laid greater stress on the art and craft of
composition than on its moral significance. This might lead one who
knows nothing else of her work to conclude that Didion is a kind of
literary aesthete for whom words on a page are their own excuse for
being. By the same token, one who knew Mother Teresa only through
her prayer life might write her off as a quietist indifferent to human
suffering. The point is that in true art, as in true religion, there is both
an inner and outer dimension. The inner workings of Didion's art make
it what it is in itself. The creative process produces the style that is her
character. However, when that style becomes incarnate in individual

verbal artifacts, it enters the public domain and, hence, the realm of
moral action. By making statements about love, sex, family, tradition,
manners, and art itself, the novels, stories, and essays of Joan Didion
not only shine with stylistic brilliance but also "display what was once
called character" (*STB* 145).

In a 1979 lecture delivered at the University of Michigan, Didion
articulates many of her long-standing views on the writing process and
adds several other provocative insights as well. She points out, for
example, that even autobiographical writers edit for coherence. The
most obvious example is telling someone a dream. "[W]e interpret the
dream as we tell it," she says, "and filter out those details which seem
to lead nowhere. We think of our dreams as stories, but they are not, at
least until we tell them."[7]

What frequently distinguishes professional writers from amateur
storytellers, and even from many scholars and critics, is their tendency
to "think of their work as a collection of objects." Whether you are
dealing with a novel, a story, or an essay, "every piece of work has its
own shape, its own texture, its own specific gravity."[8] To illustrate the
distinctiveness of the writer's perspective, Didion cites an "amiable
argument" she had with some members of the Berkeley English department about the merits of Fitzgerald's unfinished novel *The Last Tycoon.*
Although she could not disagree with any of the technical objections
her academic friends raised to the book, Didion persisted in thinking of
The Last Tycoon as "a brilliant piece of work." Then she realized what
the argument was all about:

They were looking at *The Last Tycoon* not as a fragment of a novel in progress
but as the first third of a novel for which we were simply missing the last two-
thirds. In other words they saw that first third as completed, frozen, closed—
the interrupted execution of a fully articulated plan on Fitzgerald's part—and I
saw it as something fluid, something that would change as he discovered
where the book was taking him.
. . . .
They saw the writer as someone who has a story to tell and writes it down.
I saw the writer as someone who discovers the story only in the act of
making it up.[9]

In her most nearly definitive essay on the creative process, "Why I
Write," Didion describes writing as "the act of saying *I,* of imposing

oneself on other people, of saying *listen to me, see it my way, change your mind.*[10] Even the essay's title, which she admits to having "stolen" from George Orwell, is verbally suggestive. The vowel sound in all three words of the title, Didion points out, is that of the first person singular pronoun. It is therefore appropriate that she illustrate her theories about the process of composition by recounting the circumstances that led to her own vocation as a writer.

Because of her failure to take a course in Milton, Didion had trouble graduating from Berkeley. When the English department finally agreed to give her a degree by the end of the summer if she would come down from Sacramento every Friday to talk about the cosmology of *Paradise Lost,* she would sometimes take the Greyhound bus to campus and at other times catch the Southern Pacific's City of San Francisco on the last leg of its transcontinental run. But today she admits:

I can no longer tell you whether Milton put the sun or the earth at the center of his universe in *Paradise Lost,* the central question of at least one century and a topic about which I wrote 10,000 words that summer, but I can still recall the exact rancidity of the butter in the City of San Francisco's dining car, and the way the tinted windows on the Greyhound bus cast the oil refineries around Carniquez Straits into a grayed and obscurely sinister light. In short my attention was always on the periphery, on what I could see and taste and touch, on the butter, and the Greyhound bus.[11]

During those undergraduate years Didion came to realize that she was not meant to be a "scholar" or an "intellectual." Only years later was she able to discover what she was meant to be—"Which was a writer."

Perhaps it is an indication of how thoroughly romanticism has come to dominate our thinking about such matters that Didion would assume a fundamental dissociation between abstract speculation and concrete perception. (No doubt, she would agree with William Carlos Williams that there should be "no ideas but in things.") As a result, her very method of composition borders on the visionary: Faulkner heard voices; Didion sees "pictures that shimmer."[12] She tells us that although she is not schizophrenic and does not use hallucinogenic drugs, the shimmering pictures she sees are similar to what schizophrenics and drug users see. Writing for Didion consists of finding the story that goes with a particular mental picture. And that "story" includes not just a sequence of events, but also the grammar that best articulates the meaning of those events. "The arrangement of the words matters, and the arrangement you want can be found in the picture in your mind. The picture dictates the arrangement."[13]

An example of Didion's method of composition can be found in the creative evolution of her novel *A Book of Common Prayer*. She began with two pictures in her mind. One was of a newspaper photograph of a hijacked 707 burning in the Middle East. Another was of the night view from a hotel room on the Colombian coast in which she spent a week with a paratyphoid. But "the picture that shimmered and made these other images coalesce was the Panama airport at 6 A.M."[14] Didion proceeds to describe the airport and to explain that she later made up a woman to put in the airport and a country to surround the airport and a family to rule said country. Finally, she found the proper narrative voice for her story by writing the following lines during her second week of work on the novel: "I knew why Charlotte went to the airport even if Victor did not. I knew about airports."

When these lines were written Didion had no idea where Charlotte Douglas had been or why Charlotte went to airports. Nor did the author even have a character named Victor. "*I knew why Charlotte went to the airport,*" she thought, "sounded incomplete. *I knew why Charlotte went to the airport even if Victor did not* carried a little more narrative drive."[15] Thus, she was stuck with a character named Victor and a narrator who knew both Charlotte and Victor. In order to acquaint herself with these characters and with the story in which they were involved it was necessary for Didion to write a novel. For her the act of creation is almost entirely a process of discovery.

Arts and Manners

Like a work of literature a man-made structure makes a statement and tells a story. The emotions aroused and attitudes nurtured by a public building can tell us something about the sensibility that constructed it and even about the society in which it stands. As Didion demonstrates, this is certainly true of the two California governor's homes and the J. Paul Getty Art Museum. However, her discussion of these California landmarks is finally less sociological than personal. Her encounter with these places becomes an occasion for self-revelation, and the revelation itself a way of saying "I."

The new California governor's residence (it is pointedly not called a "mansion") became a public monument before it was ever inhabited.

The house was built with private funds by friends of California governor Ronald Reagan and stood empty for eight years while Reagan's successor Jerry Brown lived in a $250-a-month apartment in Sacramento and slept on a mattress on the floor. It is a typical California ranch house in which everything is constructed to look like something else. Concrete blocks are made to "resemble" local abode, doorframes and exposed beams to "resemble" native redwood (the quotation marks are Didion's just so nobody misses her point). The house is "a monument not to colossal ego but to a weird absence of ego, a case study in the architecture of limited possibilities, insistently and malevolently 'democratic,' flattened out, mediocre and 'open' and as devoid of privacy or personal eccentricity as the lobby area in a Ramada Inn" (*WA* 69). [16]

Didion's essay, with its biblical title "Many Mansions," is not so much a glib exercise in Reagan bashing as it is a juxtaposition of the new California with the old. In this case the old is represented by the former governor's mansion, the house that Didion visited as a high school classmate of Governor Earl Warren's daughter Nina. Persons familiar with the national careers of Ronald Reagan and Earl Warren are apt to think of these men as our most conservative president and our most liberal chief justice. According to Didion's subjective evaluation, however, Warren is the man who lived in the aristocratic old house, while Reagan is the man who built the vulgar new one. Her conservatism is one of taste and temperament, not ideology.

Didion's mixture of sophisticated commentary and wistful reminiscence tells us more about herself than it does about the two houses she is describing. By projecting a complex and engaging persona she lures us into accepting her aesthetic judgments as those of the ideally sensitive observer (one who identifies herself with a Mary McCarthy character "who located America's moral decline in the disappearance of the first course" [*WA* 72]). She uses her wit to grab our attention and make her point, but leaves us with the impression that she is no smart aleck, that she cares deeply about what she is saying. Such a strategy amounts to a delicate balancing act. In "Many Mansions" it is an act that works.

In her discussion of the Getty museum, the personal dimension that we find in "Many Mansions" is missing. Instead, we have a perceptive bit of cultural criticism, which focuses on the conflict between the pseudo-populism of most contemporary art critics and the basic conservatism of the actual public. If the critical establishment believes that art should be fun and should serve as a catalyst to the untutored imagination, the general public tends to prefer art that is both remote and edifying. (The same has long been true in literature, where an aristocratic Longfellow enjoys greater *popular* appeal than a proletarian Whitman.) The Getty, a museum endowed by a rich man with middle-class tastes, was built for just such a public and has been visited by hordes of ordinary people who would not otherwise consider entering an art museum.

Among other things, this essay suggests that in her regard for tradi-tion and her abhorrence of chic, Didion (and perhaps Getty as well) is more in tune with what the masses value than are those who theorize on their behalf. Perhaps of more importance, however, is the fact that Didion and the museum are both making a critically unfashionable statement about the very nature of art and, indeed, of life itself. This statement tells us that

the past was perhaps different from the way we like to perceive it. Ancient marbles were not always attractively faded and worn. Ancient marbles once appeared just as they appear here: as strident, opulent evidence of imperial power and acquisition. Ancient murals were not always bleached and mel-lowed and "tasteful." Ancient murals once looked as they do here: as if dreamed by a Mafia don. Ancient fountains once worked and drowned out that very silence we have come to expect and want from the past. Ancient bronze once gleamed ostentatiously. The old world was once discomfitingly new, or even nouveau, as people like to say about the Getty. (*WA* 76)

The balance and antithesis in this passage and the marvellously effective repetition of the word "ancient" reveal that this is not a bourgeois defense of vulgarity but an artistically and intellectually respectable dissent from prevailing critical tastes. Since many of her readers probably hold the kinds of fashionable views she is attacking, Didion bears a burden of aesthetic proof that would not have been satisfied by a less thoughtful or a less well-written essay. Having satis-fied that burden of proof, she concludes her piece with an even more unfashionable defense of the very rich as being, in certain fundamental ways, not so different from you and me. "There is one of those peculiar social secrets at work here," Didion writes. "On the whole 'the critics' distrust great wealth, but 'the public' does not. On the whole 'the critics' subscribe to the romantic view of man's possibilities, but 'the public' does not. In the end the Getty stands above the Pacific Coast Highway as one of those odd monuments, a palpable contract between the very rich and the people who distrust them least" (*WA* 78).

The Moral Imagination

Although Joan Didion doesn't go quite as far as Edmund Burke, who thought that a thing lost half its evil by losing all its grossness, she seems to view morality as an extension of manners. Her dogmatic notions of right and wrong are based not on divine revelation nor on what she calls "the insidious ethic of conscience," but on the most fundamental social contract imaginable—what is sometimes called "wagon train morality." Like more refined notions of etiquette, wagon train morality involves a fairly rigid code of conduct, which is voluntarily adhered to and accepted as part of the rational order of the universe. The superego writ large, it allows almost no room for moral improvisation.

Didion illustrates this ethic with a story about an automobile accident in Death Valley. One night a car hit the shoulder of the road, and the young man who was driving was killed instantly. His female companion, though still alive, was bleeding internally, deep in shock. A nurse drove the girl to the nearest doctor, "185 miles across the floor of the Valley and three ranges of lethal mountain road" (*STB* 157), while the nurse's husband stayed to protect the boy's body from being torn apart by coyotes. To have done otherwise, the nurse explains, would have been "immoral." Didion tells us that this is one of the few pronouncements about morality that she does not distrust. "If we have been taught to keep our promises," she writes, "—if, in the simplest terms, our upbringing is good enough—we stay with the body, or have bad dreams" (*STB* 158).

What this amounts to is Darwinism properly understood. We are not being most Darwinian when we are most individualistic. The ethic of every-man-for-himself works against survival of the species. The human being's most triumphant adaptation to his environment has been the forming of societies, where cooperation and a division of labor have worked for the optimum benefit of the group. The spirit of rugged individualism may have caused pioneers to travel west, but the need to survive forced them to do so in primitive societies where the communal ethic reigned supreme. It was not the law but the anarchy of the jungle that reduced the Donner-Reed Party to cannibalism.

When Didion praises the virtue of self-respect, as she did in a *Vogue* essay later published in *Slouching Towards Bethlehem,* she is not talking about the kind of immature self-regard most of us lose as we get older. (For her that traumatic moment of loss came when she failed to be elected to Phi Beta Kappa and "faced myself that day with the nonplused apprehension of someone who has come across a vampire and has no crucifix at hand" [*STB* 143].) It is rather "a certain discipline, the sense that one lives by doing things one does not particularly want to do, by putting fears and doubts to one side, by weighing immediate comforts against the possibility of larger, even intangible comforts" (*STB* 145).

In looking for a model of self-respect, many observers might choose a rebel or iconoclast who challenges the established order of things. Didion goes to the other extreme and lionizes Chinese Gordon for putting on a clean white suit and holding Khartoum against the Mahdi. (One suspects that for Didion the white suit is as important here as the military action.) "To say that Waterloo was won on the playing fields of Eton," she writes, "is not to say that Napoleon might have been saved by a crash program in cricket; to give formal dinners in the rain forest would be pointless did not the candlelight flickering on the liana call forth deeper, stronger disciplines, values instilled long before. It is a kind of ritual, helping us to remember who and what we are. In order to remember it, one must have known it" (*STB* 147).

There is really no contradiction between Didion's sense that writing is a way of saying *I* and her belief in corporate morality. The society she most closely identifies with is the vanished agrarian culture of pre-World War II Sacramento. As she remembers (or perhaps reinvents) that lost world, it seems strikingly similar to the hierarchial culture of the traditional South, where people knew their place and their obligations and where life was lived according to inherited codes of behavior. Because the modern world is so different from that older vision of the good life, the culturally reactionary artist, such as Didion, becomes a misfit and an anachronism who—like the pre-Vatican II Catholic praying in Latin—espouses values no longer held by any extant community.

Chapter Three

Democratic Vistas

One of the consequences of the rise of the "new fiction" Didion casti-
gated in her essay for *National Review* was the decline of narrative
realism as the dominant mode in American letters. Along with this
alteration in literary fashion, a fundamental change in the nature of the
reading public itself occurred in the postwar era. The bourgeois audience, which had been the primary market for mimetic fiction since the
time of Samuel Richardson, was abandoning the novel for more techno-
logically advanced storytelling media, such as films and television, or
for pulp fantasy—spy thrillers, horror stories, formula romances, and
soft-core pornography.

Consequently, many writers of Didion's generation found themselves
in a bind. If their training and temperament inclined them toward the
realistic novel, they were simultaneously bucking the trend in high
literature and seeking a popular audience that no longer existed. (Narrative realists from Twain to Hemingway had been able to reach both the
critics and the people.) One solution to this impasse was to bring the
techniques of the realistic novelist to the writing of feature journalism.
What was considered an apprenticeship or a fast-buck sideline for
earlier generations of writers, who saw fiction as the higher dream, had
now become an art form in its own right. Those who want to know
what American life and literature was really like in the sixties and
seventies will find the answer in the higher journalism of the era, in the
work of such master craftsmen as Tom Wolfe, Norman Mailer, John
Gregory Dunne, Hunter S. Thompson, and Joan Didion.

No Dark and Bloodied Ground

Because she is a self-admitted "white middle-class Protestant writer,"
rather than a member of some more exotic racial, ethnic, or religious
group, Joan Didion considers herself " 'different' within the world of
letters."[1] Although this difference may have been a disadvantage during
the sixties, when various minority groups were clamoring for their niche

in American life and literature, it became less so in the seventies as the much-maligned suburban middle class began to shed its liberal guilt feelings and reassert its dominance in our cultural and political life. As the flower children became yuppies and began to raise their own children, or to regret that the rundown of the biological clock prevented them from having any, they became nostalgic for their own golden childhoods—when grandfatherly Ike was in the White House, Father knew best, and no social rebel was more dangerous than Eddie Haskell. A prime example of this nostalgia craze in American culture can be found in a special issue of *Esquire* (December 1975) devoted almost entirely to "great American things." The prologue was written by Tom Wolfe, and the various articles included "Mom," by Grace Paley; "The Flag," by Russell Baker; "Coca-Cola," by Jean Stafford; "Baseball," by Tom Wicker; "Acid Indigestion," by Art Buchwald; "TV," by Andy Warhol; "Viable Solutions," by Edwin Newman; "Bourbon," by Walker Percy; "The Corner Store," by Eudora Welty; and "The Shopping Center," by Joan Didion.

Didion's contribution, reprinted in *The White Album* as "On the Mall," opens with a litany of familiar names and half-forgotten concepts, creating the cumulative effect of "found poetry":

They float on the landscape like pyramids to the boom years, all those Plazas and Malls and Esplanades. All those Squares and Fairs. All those Towns and Dales, all those Villages, all those Forests and Parks and Lands. Stonestown. Hillsdale. Valley Fair, Mayfair, Northgate, Southgate, Eastgate, Westgate. Gulfgate. They are toy garden cities in which no one lives but everyone consumes, profound equalizers, the perfect fusion of the profit motive and the egalitarian ideal, and to hear their names is to recall the words and phrases no longer quite current. Baby Boom. Consumer Explosion. Leisure Revolution. Do-It-Yourself Revolution. Backyard Revolution. Suburbia. (*WA* 180)

As with so many of her interests, Didion's fascination with shopping centers is based as much on personal experience as intellectual curiosity. While working for *Vogue* in New York during the mid-1950s, she took a correspondence course from the University of California in shopping-center theory. (Her grand scheme was to finance her writing by planning and running a center or two.) Before it became a mere economic expedient, however, the shopping center had been for Didion part of a mythic landscape. During the postwar years of the late 1940s, "the frontier had been reinvented, and its shape was the subdivision, that new free land on which all settlers would recast their lives *tabula rasa*. For one perishable moment there the American idea seemed about to achieve itself, via F.H.A. housing and the acquisition of major appliances" (*WA* 181).

But now that the postwar boom has given way to the era of limits and the automobile has come more readily to represent a fifth mortgage than a fifth freedom, shopping centers have ceased to be the enchanted bazaars of democracy. For Didion, as for Tammy Faye Bakker, they have become temporary, interchangeable havens from the burden of being oneself. "In each of them one moves for a while in an aqueous suspension not only of light but of judgment, not only of judgment but of 'personality.' One meets no acquaintances at The Esplanade. One gets no telephone calls at Edgewater Plaza" (*WA* 186).

Like the shopping center, the freeway symbolizes an ethos of economic growth and personal mobility. A mere artery in most places, it is the very jugular of transportation in Los Angeles County—the nation's most sprawling metropolitan area. In a *White Album* essay entitled "Bureaucrats," an irate commuter named Joan Didion tilts her lance at the California state highway bureaucracy for its attempt to disrupt the rhythm of the freeway. The proximate cause of her ire is something called Diamond Lane, a traffic experiment that involved reserving the fast inner lane of the Santa Monica freeway for vehicles carrying three or more people. "[I]n practice this meant that 25 per cent of the freeway was reserved for 3 percent of the cars" (*WA* 81).

The situation Didion describes involves more than a mere case of traffic congestion. What is at issue is an ethic of "enlightened" manipulation versus one of personal autonomy. The planners in Sacramento are interested in conserving fuel and in reducing pollution. The individual driver is interested in getting where he wants to go as expeditiously as possible. Didion might have explored the philosophical implications of this conflict a bit more fully. What, for example, does the Diamond Lane slowdown tell us about the feasibility of Luddite solutions to the problems of a technological society? Have California's countercultural bureaucrats simply miscalculated the effects of their policy or do they secretly believe that snarl is beautiful? Although Didion only touches on these issues, she does evoke something of the mystique and ritual of the freeway, just as she had a few years earlier in depicting the compulsive freeway driving of Maria Wyeth in *Play It as It Lays*. "Mere driving on the freeway," Didion writes, "is in no way the same as participating in it. . . . Actual participation requires a total surrender, a concentration so intense as to seem a kind of narcosis, a rapture-of-the-freeway. The mind goes clean. The rhythm takes over" (*WA* 83).

Although Didion writes movingly and perceptively about a life and culture that is familiar to her, she is also able to enter worlds that are strange and report back in a voice that is remarkably nuanced while sounding totally objective. With Hemingway, she believes that what is left out of one's prose can frequently be as important as what is put in. Her editorial voice is almost always sensible, sometimes bordering on the profound, but what she shows us invariably is more revealing than what she tells us. This is true when she is writing of the dreamers who have come west to make a new life for themselves and of the lower-middle-class whites who inhabit what she calls "the invisible city" of Southern California. And it is even more true when her moral imagination is coming to terms with the all-too-visible counterculture of Haight-Ashbury.

Where Dreams Come True

One of the characteristics that distinguishes Southern from Northern California is that the North was originally settled by pioneers who came west in Conestoga wagons, whereas the South was not settled until the railroad was finished in the 1880s and a rate war had reduced the fare from the Missouri Valley to the West Coast to one dollar per passenger. As John Gregory Dunne notes, "What the railroad had essentially created in southern California was a frontier resort, a tumor on the western ethic. Bargain basement pioneers . . . flooded into southern California."[2] This process picked up steam as the population of greater Los Angeles increased by 1600 percent in the first four decades of our own century and exploded during the postwar boom. In her highly regarded feature article "Some Dreamers of the Golden Dream," Joan Didion writes of those who have immigrated to that part of Southern California known as San Bernardino County. "Here is the last stop for all those who came from somewhere else," she says, "for all those who drifted away from the cold and the past and the old ways. Here is where they are trying to find a new life style, trying to find it in the only places they know to look: the movies and the newspapers" (*STB* 4). One such person was Lucille Marie Maxwell Miller.

Born on 17 January 1930 in Winnipeg, Manitoba, Lucille was the only child of Seventh-Day Adventist school teachers. After a year at Walla Walla College in Washington state, she married a twenty-four-year-old dentist named Gorden ("Cork") Miller. They spent some time in Guam, where Cork finished his army duty, and in a small town in Oregon before moving to California in 1957. "By the summer of 1964 they had achieved the bigger house on the better street and the familiar accoutrements of a family on its way up: the $30,000 a year, the three children for the Christmas card, the picture window, the family room, the newspaper photographs that showed Mrs. Gordon Miller, Ontario Heart Fund Chairman . . .' " (*STB* 8–9). (The repeated use of the definite article here is a clear hint of what Didion is up to.) Also, that summer the marriage was beginning to fall apart.

By the end of the summer, however, Lucille and Cork had managed to weather talk of suicide and divorce. They were seeing a marriage counselor, contemplating a fourth child, and making a concerted effort toward reconciliation. Then, on the night of October 7, 1964, as Lucille Miller was on her way home from getting milk at a twenty-four-hour market, her Volkswagen came to a sudden stop, caught fire, and proceeded to burn. When help finally arrived, an hour and fifteen minutes later, she was sobbing and incoherent. Her husband had been asleep in the back of the Volkswagen. " 'What will I tell the children, when there's nothing left, nothing left in the casket,' she cried. . . . 'How can I tell them there's nothing left?' " (*STB* 6).

In her description of Cork Miller's funeral, Didion's instinctive sense of drama causes her to save the most important detail until last. She tells us that there were some two hundred mourners at the closed casket funeral; that they heard Elder Robert E. Denton of the Seventh-Day Adventist Church of Ontario say that for Gordon Miller there will be "no more death, no more heartaches, no more misunderstandings"; that "a light rain fell, a blessing in a dry season, and a female vocalist sang 'Safe in the Arms of Jesus.' " Only then does she tell us that "a tape recording of the service was made for the widow, who was being held without bail in the San Bernardino County Jail on a charge of first-degree murder" (*STB* 6–7).

Didion structures her treatment of this story thematically rather than chronologically. At the outset she describes the Southern California setting, narrates the basic circumstances of Cork Miller's death, and informs us of Lucille's incarceration. Only then does the author fill us in on Mrs. Miller's background and give us a more detailed account of the events of that October night. Afterward, we see the prosecution's case unfolding as the assistant district attorney argues that Lucille Miller drugged her husband and set their car on fire in order to collect his insurance money. A plausible motive emerges when it is revealed that Lucille had been having an extramarital affair with one of her neighbors. In other words, the case has all the makings of classic soap opera.

By distancing herself from her material, however, Didion avoids sensationalizing it. In fact, her language is so elegantly crafted that this piece is closer to neoclassicism than to melodrama. Like so many of the new journalists, Didion gives her story the coherence of art by employing what borders on omniscient point of view. Her omniscience, however, does not take the form of sympathetic identification with her characters (as in Hersey's *Hiroshima,* Capote's *In Cold Blood,* and Mailer's *The Executioner's Song*) but is manifest in a series of dogmatic pronouncements that reflect aristocratic disdain for those characters. As a rule, dogmatism and snobbishness do not make for an attractive ethos, but it is a measure of Didion's success as a stylist that we ignore those ostensible handicaps. Whatever the personal anguish of the Miller family may have been, it seems to have been worth it to have inspired Joan Didion to write "Some Dreamers of the Golden Dream."

Didion's dogmatism gains credibility from her skillful mixture of objective facts and critical opinions. In one sentence we read about the divorce rate and the density of trailer homes in San Bernardino County, and in the next we encounter generalizations about the history and psychology of an entire class of people. In both cases the voice is of someone who sounds as if she knows what she's talking about. She also knows how to say things in a way that appeals to sensibility as well as sense. When she talks about the Millers' attempts at reconciliation, for example, she says that they had resigned "themselves to cutting their losses and their hopes" (*STB* 9). By predicating two nouns with the same verb, Didion describes this situation with a zeugma, one of the favorite rhetorical devices of Alexander Pope. The point is to use syntax as a means of conveying ironic juxtaposition. This Didion does brilliantly as a way of commenting on marriages gone bad.

Moreover, she seems to have an unerring sense for the right visual detail. We come away from this story remembering that the crowds trying to get into the Lucille Miller trial would begin forming at 6 A.M. and that "college girls camped at the courthouse all night, with stores of graham crackers and No-Cal" (*STB* 20). We recall the scene in the courtroom when the guilty verdict is brought in. As Lucille's friend Sandy Slagle screams hysterically at the jurors, "sheriff's deputies moved in . . . , each wearing a string tie that read '1965 SHERIFF'S RODEO.' " And then there is jail itself—the California Institution for Women at Frontera:

Cattle graze across the road, and Rainbirds sprinkle the alfalfa. Frontera has a softball field and tennis courts, and looks as if it might be a California junior college, except that the trees are not yet high enough to conceal the concertina wire around the top of the Cyclone fence. On visitor's day there are big cars in the parking area, big Buicks and Pontiacs that belong to grandparents and sisters and fathers (not many of them belong to husbands) and some of them have bumper stickers that say "SUPPORT YOUR LOCAL POLICE." (*STB* 25)

What we do not come away from this story with is any clear sense of whether Lucille Miller actually murdered her husband. This may be because Joan Didion, unlike the jurors in the case, has a reasonable doubt concerning Lucille's guilt. But it may also be that in the deeply mechanistic world Didion describes, one's fate is set without regard to guilt or innocence. (We do not know, for example, whether the women in prison receive no visits from their husbands because the husbands have abandoned them or because they have knocked the husbands off.) Those who dream the golden dream will end up paying for their delusions. They are victims—whether of an unjust court decision or of a distorted worldview spawned by tabloid romance is finally beside the point. And yet the dream continues. Didion completes her story not with the incarcerated Lucille but with news of Lucille's former lover, Arthwell Hayton, who marries his children's governess, a Swedish beauty named Wenche Berg (would a fiction writer have dared to make these names up?). The description of the bride's outfit brings the story to a close with two words that perfectly capture Didion's message: "A coronet of seed pearls held her illusion veil" (*STB* 28).

The Invisible City

The year is 1968, and Elder Robert J. Theobold, pastor of the Friendly Bible Apostolic Church—Port Hueneme, California—has received direct word from the Almighty of an impending earthquake. As a result, he and his followers plan to pull up stakes and relocate in Murfreesboro, Tennessee, an area of infrequent earth tremors. In the

first section of a *White Album* sequence entitled "Notes Toward a
Dreampolitik," Joan Didion tells us of her visit with Brother Theobold
and his flock.

What Didion gives us in this sketch is a slice of the exotic religious
life of Southern California. In Nathanael West's *The Day of the Locust,*
Evelyn Waugh's *The Loved One,* and much other fiction, we read of the
various cults and sects that flourish out there in what Didion calls "the
interior wilderness," where the actual wilderness has come to an end.
And yet, these works are, if anything, less implausible than the reality
they are satirizing. (What novelist, for example, would have concocted
a story as bizarre as that of Jim Jones and the People's Temple?) Didion
is acutely interested in this phenomenon (witness her emphasis on
Lucille Miller's Seventh-Day Adventist background), apparently seeing
inner-light fundamentalism as simply one version of the golden dream.
However, she is sensitive enough to the possibilities of her material not
to strain for effect. By merely allowing her subjects to speak for themselves, she is able to achieve an ironic juxtaposition of the Cities of God
and Man. Brother Theobold, for example, says to the author: "From the
natural point of view I didn't care to go to Murfreesboro at all. . . . We
just bought this place, it's the nicest place we ever had. But I put it up
to the Lord, and the Lord said *put it up for sale.* Care for a Dr. Pepper?"
(*WA* 98).

When Didion enters the picture to speak in her own voice, she
comments perceptively on what the Pentecostal sects tell her about our
common culture (or lack thereof). "In the social conventions by which
we now live," she writes, "there is no category for people like Brother
Theobold and his congregation, most of whom are young and white
and nominally literate. . . . They participate in the national anxieties
only through a glass darkly" (*WA* 98). (Just in case anyone missed the
point, these are not Joan Didion's kind of people.) "It is no coinci-
dence," she concludes, "that the Pentecostal churches have their strongest hold in places where Western civilization has its most superficial
hold. There are more than twice as many Pentecostal as Episcopal
churches in Los Angeles" (*WA* 99).

The next stop in Didion's exploration of the dreampolitik takes her
to movie theaters showing motorcycle exploitation films, or bike movies. She attended nine of these films during a single week in 1970 and
concluded that this "underground folk literature for adolescents" was
telling her "some news I was not getting from the *New York Times*"
(*WA* 100, 101). In what Robert Sklar calls "movie-made America," the

fantasies of popular culture can be valuable source material for the social historian. To Didion's mind, bike movies are nothing less than "ideograms" of a future in which "a nonexistent frustration threshold is seen not as psychopathic but as a 'right' " (*WA* 101).

Although Didion does not make this point, bike movies may well represent an alarming extension of the American tendency to romanticize the outlaw. Originally, a certain revisionism was necessary to make thugs such as Jesse James, Billy the Kid, and Pretty Boy Floyd into folk heroes. They had to be good boys who were wronged by society, who remained invariably polite to all women, and who were particularly devoted to their mothers. The makers of bike movies (Roger Corman et al.) have abandoned this transparent hypocrisy not because of their superior honesty, but because gratuitous mayhem is, for their audience, the point of the exercise. According to Didion, this audience consists of "boys who majored in shop and worked in gas stations and later held them up . . . , children of vague 'hill' stock who grew up absurd in the West and Southwest, children whose whole lives are an obscure grudge against a world they think they never made." These kids may be part of an "invisible city," but they are "increasingly everywhere, and their style is that of an entire generation" (*WA* 101).

We should not assume, however, that Didion regards all movie-made fantasies as psychopathic. In her continuing look at the fringes of society she next focuses on a remarkably benign and endearing cinema addict—the unknown actress Dallas Beardsley. In many ways Dallas resembles the starstruck young dreamers who populate countless Hollywood novels (one thinks of Faye Greener and Todd Hackett in Nathanael West's *The Day of the Locust*, of the marathon dancers in Horace McCoy's *They Shoot Horses, Don't They?*, and of Mona Matthews and Ralph Carston in McCoy's *I Should Have Stayed Home*). Dallas is a twenty-two-year-old woman who has spent her entire life in Southern California, yearning for motion picture fame. "There is no one like me in the world," she declares in a full-page advertisement on the fifth page of *Daily Variety*, "I'm going to be a movie star" (*WA* 102).

The sophisticate in Joan Didion realizes how anachronistic this young woman's ambition is. Wanting to be a movie star was no longer a fantasy even of inveterate moviegoers. (When Didion and Dunne decided, a few years later, to write a remake of *A Star Is Born*, they set it not in the world of motion pictures but in the music industry.) But this fact seemed not to faze Dallas Beardsley. Even though she could read about the wretched lives of flesh-and-blood movie stars in the supermar-

ket tabloids, her idea of cinematic fame seemed right out of the original
A Star Is Born (the one with Janet Gaynor). To her stardom meant
"bringing my family a bunch of presents on Christmas Day, you know,
like carloads, and putting them by the tree. And it means happiness,
and living by the ocean in a huge house." But the most important thing
was to be known: "It's important to me to be *known*" (*WA* 103).

As she drove home that day, Didion realized how far removed her
own notions of Hollywood were from the dreams that obsessed Dallas
Beardsley and others like her. What is commendable is that she
refuses to condescend to the Dallas Beardsleys of this world or hold
them up as objects of ridicule. Perhaps Didion is enough of a romantic to understand what makes such people tick and enough of a realist
to know that the sort of convention that equates wanting to be a
movie star not with the golden dream but with a trip to the UCLA
neuropsychiatric ward is itself a myth (or antimyth) of success. Knowing all of this allows her to celebrate the original myth as at least a
fiction worthy of respect. "In the invisible city," she concludes, "girls
were still disappointed at not being chosen cheerleader. In the invisible city girls still got discovered at Schwab's and later met their true
loves at the Mocambo or the Troc, still dreamed of big houses by the
ocean and carloads of presents by the Christmas tree, still prayed to be
known" (*WA* 104).

Didion brings her "Notes Toward a Dreampolitik" to a close with a
quick cinematic cut to a Gamblers Anonymous meeting in Gardena,
California, "draw-poker capital of Los Angeles County" (*WA* 104). Her
description of this meeting is a shortened version of a *Saturday Evening
Post* column entitled "Getting Serenity." Unlike Didion's sensitive
treatment of Dallas Beardsley, that original column was supercilious
and elitist in tone. In effect, Didion was taking a cheap shot at some
rather inarticulate but troubled people, compulsive gamblers who were
trying to reform themselves through mutual self-help. However, in the
revised version of this sketch, she eschews editorial comment, giving us
instead only a cinema verité glimpse of the recovering gamblers. The
latter approach is more effective, if only because it is less snide and
judgmental.

The other three pieces in this "Dreampolitik" sequence seemed to me
to have worked better in their original, separate versions. Although the
juxtapositions are suggestive, they are not themselves sufficient to
make a series of fragments fit coherently together. But at least Didion
has made the effort to tour a world far different from her own. The

lower-middle-class inhabitants of Southern California are not the landed gentry of Sacramento or the beautiful people of Malibu. (Neither, as we shall see, are they the hippies of the Haight-Ashbury or the crazed murderers of Cielo Drive.) They are what, in another section of the country, might be called "poor white trash." They are people the media generally ignore.

Helter Skelter

"Many people I know in Los Angeles believe that the Sixties ended abruptly on August 9, 1969, ended at the exact moment when word of the murders on Cielo Drive traveled like brushfire through the community, and in a sense this is true. The tension broke that day. The paranoia was fulfilled" (*WA* 47). The murders being referred to are those of Sharon Tate Polanski, Abigail Folger, Jay Sebring, Voytek Frykowski, Steven Parent, and Rosemary and Leno LaBianca; and the passage itself is fairly typical of the title essay of *The White Album*.[3] This essay consists of fifteen loosely connected scenes from the late 1960s, scenes that include matters of public concern—such as the activities of Huey Newton and the Black Panthers and the student rebellion at San Francisco State College—and moments of private crisis in the author's own life. Didion is attempting, through the mood of physical and psychic violence that pervades these fifteen scenes, to convey a sense of American life at a particular historical moment.

We learn, for example, that the author avidly studied the trial of the Ferguson brothers—killers of silent screen star Ramon Novarro—and that she came to know Manson follower Linda Kasabian rather well. For Didion these names have a kind of totemic significance. For her they seem to represent American culture as a whole in the late 1960s. However, this fact may tell us less about the sixties themselves than it does about a kind of Malibu provincialism that occasionally creeps into Didion's writing. Three weeks before the Tate-LaBianca murders, Teddy Kennedy drove off the bridge at Chappaquiddick and Neil Armstrong bounded onto the surface of the moon—two events that might have represented the end of the sixties for most other Americans.

In addition to narrowness of sensibility, there are also structural problems here. Early in the essay Didion says, "We live entirely, especially if we are writers, by the imposition of a narrative line upon disparate images, by the 'ideas' with which we have learned to freeze the shifting phantasmagoria which is our actual experience" (*WA* 11).

What she has given us in "The White Album," however, is not a narrative line but the "disparate images" and "shifting phantasmagoria" themselves. Although many interesting lines of development are suggested, none is really followed through. To be sure, the fragmentation is intentional. (As Robert Towers points out in his review of *The White Album*, Didion "gives the impression of having refined [her personal neurosis] to the point where it vibrates in exquisite attunement to the larger craziness of the world she inhabits and observes."[4]) But the effect is what critics used to call the "fallacy of imitative form," which is sort of like writing about boredom in a boring way.

I suspect that this essay would have been more effective had Didion's focus been less diffuse, had she not left us wanting to know so much more about the Fergusons and Linda Kasabian. To begin to appreciate the possibilities that go undeveloped here, one need only consider the author's achievement in "Some Dreamers of the Golden Dream." In that essay, unlike "The White Album," she does in fact impose narrative order on the phantasmagoria of actual experience.

I do not mean to suggest that "The White Album" is without redeeming merit. Here, as elsewhere, Didion demonstrates a capacity for engaging our interest. (Indeed, her very stylistic virtues—by raising our expectations of everything she writes—can lead to unreasonable disappointment in work that is less than her best.) Unfortunately, she has allowed that interest to dissipate by sacrificing coherence for the sake of scope. Perhaps the only way to avoid such a pitfall is to find a story that can also serve as a cultural synecdoche. The next essay we will consider accomplishes that very task.

The title piece of *Slouching Towards Bethlehem* is one of Joan Didion's most famous journalistic efforts. In addition to being a vivid and powerful description of life in Haight-Ashbury, it raises broader questions about the cultural matrix from which Haight-Ashbury was spawned. As Didion indicates in her preface, "I was talking about something more general than a handful of children wearing mandalas on their foreheads" (*STB* xiv). And yet, many readers missed all but the most obvious and tangential aspects of Didion's analysis. (She tells us that "disc jockeys telephoned my house and wanted to discuss [on the air] the incidence of 'filth' in the Haight-Ashbury, and acquaintances congratulated me on having finished the piece 'just in time,' because 'the whole fad's dead now, *fini, kaput*' " [*STB* iv].) For some the essay's very timeliness may have obscured Didion's more serious intentions.

The author begins by describing American culture in the mid-1960s in terms resembling Yeats's prophetic poem "The Second Coming" (from which Didion derives her title). (In this culture, where the center was not holding, "adolescents drifted from city to torn city, sloughing off both the past and the future as snakes shed their skins, children who were never taught and would never now learn the games that had held the society together" [*STB* 84].) Most of the rest of "Slouching Towards Bethlehem" consists of an accumulation—actually a montage—of short, fragmented scenes. Formalistically, Didion is doing here what she would later do in *Play It as It Lays* and *A Book of Common Prayer:* she shapes the printed page in such a way that its very appearance gives us a subliminal message about the story she is telling. For the most part, this story is told in a large number of relatively short paragraphs, with quite a few shifts in scene and very little overt narrative connection. Thus the reading experience itself conveys a sense of fragmentation. However, the general consistency of ambience and mood and Didion's own artistic control are so nearly complete that these fragments form a larger mosaic; we are never lost in the incoherence of imitative form.

Although Didion is striving for cumulative effect, several individual descriptions and bits of dialogue are particularly memorable. One recalls, for example, Max and Sharon—a young couple who "plan to leave for Africa and India, where they can live off the land. 'I got this trust fund, see,' Max says, 'which is useful in that is tells cops and border patrols I'm O.K., but living off the land is the thing. You can get your high and your dope in the city, O.K., but we gotta get out somewhere and live organically' " (*STB* 96). Obviously, Max and Sharon are not aware that Indians and Africans themselves find it difficult to live off the land, that the material largesse of America—which hippies supposedly repudiate—is frequently the only thing standing between these foreign peoples and mass starvation. But such considerations are too mundane to trouble the flower children; their minds are focused on more ethereal concerns. For example, a young man named Steve asserts: "I found love on acid. But I lost it. And now I'm finding it again. With nothing but grass" (*STB* 97).

One also recalls the terse clarity and precision with which Didion describes a nonparticipant's view of an acid trip. "At three-thirty that afternoon," she writes, "Max, Tom, and Sharon placed tabs under their tongues and sat down together in the living room to wait for the flash. Barbara stayed in the bedroom, smoking hash. During the next four hours a window banged once in Barbara's room, and about five-thirty some children had a fight in the street. A curtain billowed in the afternoon wind. A cat scratched a beagle in Sharon's lap. Except for the sitar music on the stereo there was no other sound or movement until seven-thirty, when Max said 'Wow' " (*STB* 106).

And then there is the author's dispassionate account of the lives of Haight-Ashbury's youngest inhabitants. We read of a boy named Michael who amuses himself by burning joss sticks and by sitting on a rocking horse whose paint is worn off. Michael is "a very blond and pale and dirty child," and the first time Didion saw him he was sitting on that rocking horse in a blue theatrical spotlight, "crooning softly to the wooden horse. Michael is three years old. He is a bright child but does not yet talk" (*STB* 95). Another child, age five, is named Susan. When Didion first encounters her, she is sitting "on the living-room floor, wearing a reefer coat, reading a comic book. She keeps licking her lips in concentration and the only off thing about her is that she's wearing white lipstick. . . . For a year now her mother has given her both acid and peyote. Susan describes it as getting stoned" (*STB* 127, 128).

Finally, the last paragraph of "Slouching Towards Bethlehem" is a tour de force, an eloquently symbolic ideogram of the moral pathology that pervades Haight-Ashbury:

Sue Ann's three-year-old Michael started a fire this morning before anyone was up, but Don got it out before much damage was done. Michael burned his arm though, which is probably why Sue Ann was so jumpy when she happened to see him chewing on an electric cord. "You'll fry like rice," she screamed. The only people around were Don and one of Sue Ann's macrobiotic friends and somebody who was on his way to a commune in the Santa Lucias, and they didn't notice Sue Ann screaming at Michael because they were in the kitchen trying to retrieve some very good Moroccan hash which had dropped down through a floorboard damaged in the fire. (*STB* 128)

Although the praise this essay has received is amply deserved, one can still suggest a few critical reservations. To begin with, Didion's objective, camera-eye narration may have drawbacks as well as advantages. Since the hippies all seem interchangeable, the accumulation of scene upon scene begins—after a while—to become repetitive. Moreover, the author's sociological analysis, though discerning, is not well enough integrated into the essay. Coming at the beginning of the piece, it promises the kind of authorial voice that worked so well in "Some Dreamers of the Golden Dream" and then disappears, like Hemingway's iceberg,[5] beneath the surface of the story. Either omniscience or invisibility would have worked as a narrative stance much better than an uncertain combination of the two. A way out of the impasse might have been for Didion to inject herself more into the piece. (She tells us that she wrote this essay at a time of personal distress, when her own center was not holding; yet her persona is decidedly low-profile, as if she were just another reporter or—in the argot of Haight-Ashbury— a "media poisoner.") The title essay of *The White Album* is most affecting when the pathetic fallacy is most evident.

Ultimately, though, we must judge a writer's work by what is there, not by what might have been there. Perhaps we would even be wise to adopt a critical standard that Didion herself suggests in the preface of *Slouching Towards Bethlehem,* where she tells us that certain lines from Yeats's "The Second Coming" have reverberated in her inner ear "as if they were surgically implanted there" (*STB* xiii). The visual images from Didion's essay continue to do much the same thing to our inner eye, more than two decades after the disc jockeys stopped calling her home and the flower children themselves became not just a lost but a forgotten generation.

Chapter Four
The Center Cannot Hold

On several occasions Joan Didion has commented on her aversion to politics. (In 1979 she told Michiko Kakutani that she had voted in 1964 [for Goldwater] but only twice since then.[1]) For example, she said to Sara Davidson in 1977, "I never had faith that the answers to human problems lay in anything that could be called political. I thought the answers, if there were answers, lay someplace in man's soul."[2] We should not conclude, however, that Didion is indifferent to public issues, only that her political opinions run counter to conventional ideology. Such ideology, on both the Right and the Left, consists of strange mixtures of authoritarianism and anarchism. For the most part, the right advocates strong government action in the areas of domestic law enforcement and national defense but supports only limited government interference in the marketplace. In contrast, the left sees the proper function of government in approximately opposite terms. Didion, however, would probably concur with Thoreau that "that government is best which governs not at all."

She told Davidson: "The ethic I was raised in was specifically a Western frontier ethic. That means being left alone and leaving others alone. . . . The politics I personally want are anarchic. Throw out the laws. Tear it down. Start all over. That is very romantic because it assumes that, left to their own devices, people would do good things for one another. I doubt that that's true. But I would like to believe it."[3] In point of fact, Didion's view of human nature is anything but sanguine. She seems to believe, however, that our *individual* foibles and cruelties are to be preferred to the systematized evils of group action. According to such a view, the surest way to make things worse is to organize for the purpose of making them better. Because of the evenhandedness of her anarchism, Didion has little good to say about political movements of any ideological stripe. She is a partisan not of causes but of the individual's right to be left alone.

Vanity Fair

In her *Slouching Towards Bethlehem* essay "Comrade Laski CPUSA (M-L)" and three sections of the title essay to *The White Album*, Didion exposes with understated irony the vanities lying behind so much of the radical politics of the sixties. The first of these pieces focuses on the Old Left in the person of a twenty-six-year-old UCLA dropout who has found in a revolutionary Maoist sect the same sense of cosmic purpose that drives the Brother Theobolds of this world. The more recent selections are topical considerations of an aspect of the counterculture largely unexplored in "Slouching Towards Bethlehem"—the carnival-like politics of the New Left.

Like so many fringe groups on the Left, Michael Laski's cult—the Communist Party USA (Marxist-Leninist)—seems less concerned with overthrowing American capitalism than in questioning the ideological soundness of other true believers. This includes the traditional American Communist Party, which is a "revisionist bourgeois clique"; the Progressive Labor Party, the Trotskyites, and "the revisionist clique headed by Gus Hall"—all of which have proven themselves "opportunistic bourgeois lackeys by making their peace appeal not to the 'workers' but to the liberal imperialists"; and, last but not least, H. Rap Brown, who is "the tool, if not the conscious agent, of the ruling imperialist class" (STB 61–62).

Didion chooses to view Laski's particular mania more in psychological and metaphysical than in doctrinal terms. She even feels a certain affinity with those whose "dread is so acute that they turn to extreme and doomed commitments." She can "appreciate the elaborate systems with which some people manage to fill the void, appreciate all the opiates of the people, whether they are as accessible as alcohol and heroin and promiscuity or as hard to come by as faith in God or History" (*STB* 63).

Didion completes her visit with Comrade Laski by describing one of the party's daily rituals—Comrade Simmons's report on the day's receipts from sale of the revolutionary tabloid *People's Voice*. When queried about the paucity of his take, Simmons explains that business is always bad the day before welfare and unemployment checks arrive. "You see what the world of Michael Laski is," Didion concludes, "a minor but perilous triumph of being over nothingness" (*STB* 66).

In turning her attention from the Old to the New Left, Didion moves from the somber to the festive or, to paraphrase Jerry Rubin, from Karl to Groucho Marx. "The White Album" deals with the 1960s, a time when a vocal segment of the baby boom generation discovered that protesting war abroad and injustice at home was not only a feel-good pastime but, when properly done, more fun than a panty raid. All that was needed were flamboyant role models with the proper revolutionary credentials. Few played the part more brilliantly than Huey P. Newton and the Black Panthers.

Named for Huey P. Long, the Louisiana populist who called himself the Kingfish after a character on the "Amos 'n Andy" radio program, Newton was a self-taught ghetto Marxist (what the French would call an autodidact) with a flair for theatrics. Taking full advantage of the constitutional right to keep and bear arms, Newton formed a paramilitary group called the Black Panther Party and fought the Oakland, California, police in a series of pitched battles that eventually resulted in his being arrested for first-degree murder. It was at that point that Newton and the Panthers became folk heroes to campus radicals, who organized "Free Huey" rallies (Didion correctly intuits that by now Huey's actual guilt or innocence had become largely irrelevant) and displayed posters showing the head Panther sitting in an African fan chair, in black leather jacket and beret, holding a spear in one hand and a rifle in the other.

Unfortunately, Didion makes the mistake of portraying Huey Newton as a naive young man who was being manipulated by wilier (and presumably whiter) partisans of the Left, or, to use her own comparison, a latter-day Scottsboro boy. What Didion fails to perceive in Huey Newton is the sort of cunning that permitted *him* to manipulate the guilt feelings of white liberals, the romanticism of campus radicals, and the show business interests of the major news media. When Newton arrived early one morning at the emergency room of the Kaiser Foundation Hospital in Oakland with a bullet wound in his stomach, he was initially denied admittance because of his failure to produce a card proving his membership in the hospital's pre-paid health plan. Didion immediately interpreted this incident as an example of Newton's helplessness—"a collision of cultures, a classic instance of an historical outsider confronting the established order at its most petty and impenetrable level." Only later did she learn that "Huey Newton was in fact an enrolled member of the Kaiser Foundation Health Plan," or, in the words of emergency room nurse Corrine Leonard, "a Kaiser" (WA 33).

Didion seems considerably more in her element when visiting the apartment of Huey's Panther colleague Eldridge Cleaver. It is true that before being admitted to the Cleaver domain, she had to ring the apartment and stand out in the middle of the street to pass inspection. But once inside, she engaged in shop talk with Cleaver about the commercial prospects for his forthcoming book *Soul on Ice.* "It was a not unusual discussion between writers," she notes, "with the difference that one of the writers had his parole officer there and the other had stood out on Oak Street and been visually frisked before coming inside" (*WA* 34).

It is when she is describing the student strike at San Francisco State College, however, that Didion has the surest control of her material. She treats the whole spectacle as a lark, comparing it in the original version of her essay (published in the *Saturday Evening Post*) to a college musical that lacked only Peter Lawford and June Allyson. Refusing to take the protests seriously, either as idealistic struggle or threat to the body politic, she recalls a note she saw scrawled on the door of the campus cafeteria one morning: "Adjet-prop committee meeting in the Redwood Room." Didion concludes that "only someone who needed very badly to be alarmed could respond with force to a guerrilla band that not only announced its meetings on the enemy's bulletin board but seemed innocent of the spelling, and so the meaning, of the words it used" (*WA* 38).

What Didion was witnessing were "scenes of industrious self-delusion" of the sort one might find in an Evelyn Waugh novel (*WA* 39). She describes, for example, the members of the campus Students for a Democratic Society listening to a student who had driven up the peninsula to San Francisco that day from the College of San Mateo, a junior college that was located in one of the wealthiest counties in California. They hear him say: "I came up here today with some Third World students to tell you that we're with you, and we hope you'll be with *us* when we try to pull off a strike next week, because we're really into it, we carry our motorcycle helmets all the time, can't think, can't go to class. . . . I'm here to tell you that at College of San Mateo we're living like *revolutionaries*" (*WA* 40–41).

The Liberal Imagination

It probably would not have been possible for a woman as prominent as Joan Didion to write about American culture in the late sixties and early seventies without defining her position on women's liberation. In doing so, however, she poses a problem for committed feminists. As an example of someone who has so conspicuously made it in a man's world, Didion is a living testament to the metaphysical equality of women. But her sensibility as a Western loner and her constitutional aversion to cant and jargon put her at odds with *organized* feminism. As she sees it, the women's movement—like all other "radical" causes in American history—is merely a struggle for personal self-fulfillment clothed in revolutionary rhetoric. As such, it is a classic example of liberal fantasy.

Traditionally, Didion argues, the have-nots of our society have "aspired mainly to having" (*WA* 110). Once a disadvantaged group got its share of the American pie, it became part of the establishment rather than a vanguard of the proletariat. (One might argue that the failure of socialism to gain a permanent foothold in American politics is due to the *widespread* benefits of capitalism within the American economy.) So, at the moment when there seemed no group left to play the proletariat, "along came the women's movement, and the invention of women as a 'class' " (*WA* 110).

Didion applauds the novelty of "this instant transfiguration" as being "at once so pragmatic and so visionary, so precisely Emersonian, that it took the breath away, exactly confirmed one's idea of where nineteenth-century transcendental instincts, crossed with a late reading of Engels and Marx, might lead" (*WA* 110–11). The reason she finds herself at odds with feminism, then, is not its lack of political daring but its resistance to moral ambiguity. "To believe in 'the greater good,' " she writes, "is to operate, necessarily, in a certain ethical suspension. Ask anyone committed to Marxist analysis how many angels on the head of a pin, and you will be asked in return to never mind the angels, tell me who controls the production of pins" (*WA* 112).

Didion also argues that—contrary to popular misconceptions—not all feminists are hard and resourceful. Some, she tells us, even write of "the intolerable humiliations of being observed by construction workers on Sixth Avenue." Such a grievance "seemed always to take on unexplored Ms. Scarlett overtones, suggestions of fragile cultivated flowers being 'spoken to,' and therefore violated, by uppity proles" (*WA* 113). (Of course, the original *Miss* Scarlett would have used her natural feminine wiles to gain ownership of the construction company and had the proles waiting on her hand and foot.) Much the same sensibility can be discerned in lesbian literature, with its "emphasis on the superior 'tenderness' of the relationship, the 'gentleness' of the sexual connection, as if the participants were wounded birds." This ultimately leads Didion to envisioning "several million women too delicate to deal at any level with an overtly heterosexual man" (*WA* 116).

"It was a long way," Didion concludes, "From Simone de Beauvoir's grave and awesome recognition of women's role as 'the Other' to the notion that the first step in changing that role was Alix Kates Shulman's marriage contract ('wife strips beds, husband remakes them'), a document reproduced in *Ms.*, but it was toward just such trivialization that the women's movement seemed to be heading" (*WA* 113). As if to confirm this trend, Susan Braudy, in an otherwise favorable piece on Didion published in *Ms.*, confessed to finding Didion's views on feminism "almost impossible to understand."[4]

Intellectual obtuseness and self-delusion are, of course, not qualities exclusive to the women's movement, as these traits can be found anywhere. The pretensions of political activists, however, seem to be a particularly apt target for ridicule, if only because those pretensions are usually grander in design than the ones harbored by ordinary people. For example, their detractors argue that limousine liberals are really elitists who find that identifying with the plight of the dispossessed is the surest way to feel morally superior to the slightly possessed. For every Mother Teresa or Albert Schweitzer who actually bears the white man's burden, there are scores of Leonard Bernsteins waiting to give cocktail parties for the Black Panthers.

Thus far, the elitist liberal's capacity for self-parody has been ample enough to inspire polemicists such as William Buckley and social critics such as Tom Wolfe. (Wolfe's 1970 essays "Radical Chic" and "Mau-Mauing the Flak Catchers" have become minor classics of antiestablishment satire.) Some of Joan Didion's journalism of the sixties not only falls into this category but also seems to prefigure both the tone and thesis of Wolfe's better known and more controversial works. This is particularly true of her description of a visionary West Coast "think tank" in *Slouching Towards Bethlehem* and of the political activism of movie stars in *The White Album*.

The first of these essays ("California Dreaming") focuses on Santa Barbara's Center for the Study of Democratic Institutions. A sort of floating seminar, the center "is supported on the same principle as a vanity press. People who are in a position to contribute large sums of money are encouraged to participate in clarifying the basic issues" of the day (*STB* 77). The driving force behind this project is former University of Chicago president Dr. Robert M. Hutchins, an educator

who once tried to catalog "The 102 Great Ideas of Western Man." At
his think tank Hutchins fosters a kind of reverse intellectual snobbism.
"The place is in fact avidly anti-intellectual," Didion tells us, "the
deprecatory use of words like 'egghead' and 'ivory tower' reaching
heights matched only in a country-club locker room. Hutchins takes
pains to explain that by 'an intellectual community' he does not mean a
community 'whose members regard themselves as "intellectual" ' "
(*STB* 76).

On a given day in the center one might encounter founding member
Dinah Shore discussing civil rights with Bayard Rustin or hear founding member Kirk Douglas speak "his piece on 'The Arts in a Democratic Society' " (*STB* 77). Then there is "concerned citizen" Jack
Lemmon. " 'Apropos of absolutely nothing,' Mr. Lemmon says, pulling on a pipe, 'just for my own amazement—I don't *know,* but I *want* to
know—.' At this juncture he wants to know about student unrest, and,
at another, he worries that government contracts will corrupt 'pure
research' " (*STB* 77–78). Concerned citizen Paul Newman muses:
" 'You mean maybe they get a grant to develop some new kind of
plastic,' . . . and Mr. Lemmon picks up the cue: 'What happens then to
the humanities?' " (*STB* 78).

For a much fuller description of politically concerned celebrities, we
need only turn to Didion's discussion of liberal Hollywood, a community whose public life "comprises a kind of dictatorship of good intentions, a social contract in which actual and irreconcilable disagreement
is as taboo as failure or bad teeth, a climate devoid of irony" (*WA* 86–
87). It is also a climate in which one can hear once or twice a week "that
no man is an island . . . , quite often from people who think they are
quoting Ernest Hemingway" (*WA* 86).

The original version of this essay was occasioned by Didion's visit to
a Beverly Hills nightclub called Eugene's, which was run by supporters
of Senator Eugene McCarthy's 1968 campaign for the Democratic presidential nomination. Not unlike that campaign itself, Eugene's "had a
certain *deja-vu* aspect to it, a glow of 1952 humanism, . . . [recalling a
time] when everyone who believed in the Family of Man bought Scandi-
navian stainless-steel flatware and voted for Adlai Stevenson." It was at
Eugene's that Didion "heard the name 'Erich Fromm' for the first time
in a long time, and many other names cast out for the sympathetic
magic they might work" (including, as if to anticipate Wolfe's *Radical
Chic,* "Mrs. Leonard Bernstein") (*WA* 87).

What gives Hollywood liberalism a kind of surreal quality is that in the movies social problems are invariably seen in terms of a scenario: "Marlon Brando does not, in a well-plotted motion picture, picket San Quentin in vain. . . . If Budd Schulberg goes into Watts and forms a Writers' Workshop, then 'Twenty Young Writers' must emerge from it, because the scenario in question is the familiar one about how the ghetto teems with raw talent and vitality" (*WA* 88–89). Were Didion to update this essay, she might well have some interesting things to say about what it means to have a *conservative* movie actor in the White House (e.g., if arms are sold to Iranian moderates, American hostages must be released). But I suspect that her basic point would be unchanged: life in all its complexity lacks the coherence and resolution of a well-edited film.

Betrayed by History

Although conservatives also deal in social scenarios that can be just as vain and irrelevant as those of their brethren on the Left, Didion did not focus her critical scrutiny on the organized political right until her 1987 book *Miami*. Nevertheless, one can find in her earlier journalism a skepticism about many of the cherished assumptions of those Americans Richard Nixon dubbed "the great silent majority." On the whole, though, these pieces lack the critical bite of Didion's antiliberal writings. One has the sense that Didion sees herself as a silent majoritarian who no longer goes to the Episcopal Church or votes Republican but who would not think of adopting another religious or political creed. (When asked if he had ever considered becoming a Protestant, James Joyce said that he had lost his faith but not his self-respect.) As a conservative alumna, Didion can identify more with the sort of person she has ceased to be than with one she will never become.

Although she wrote perceptively about America in the sixties, Didion said remarkably little about the two political watersheds of that era—civil rights and the Vietnam War. While the silence on race continues (her piece on Huey Newton being tangential to the real issues of the black struggle), Didion's 1984 novel *Democracy* begins to suggest her attitude toward the Vietnam War. Since I discuss that novel and what it says about Vietnam in a later chapter, I mention it here only to note that it casts some retrospective light on Didion's earlier, more oblique, treatments of the Vietnam experience.[5] In particular, she seems to regard Hawaii (which is the primary setting of *Democracy*) as the proper vantage point from which to view America's involvement in

Southeast Asia. Not only is it our most Asian state—so far west that it is east—but it was also the site of America's tragic humiliation at Pearl Harbor. Moreover, in the late sixties and early seventies, some of the casualties from Vietnam were buried in the National Memorial Cemetery of the Pacific, a military graveyard located in an extinct volcano called Punchbowl, not far from Honolulu. (Although most of these were Island boys, a few were brought back across the Pacific by their families from the Mainland.) In a 1970 column for *Life*, later published in *The White Album*, Didion describes the burial of one such casualty.

Rather than writing an antiwar polemic, Didion uses a beautifully austere prose to say something about the individual human costs of armed conflict. She begins with a faintly ironic portrait of the superintendent of Punchbowl, Martin T. Corley—an efficient and self-satisfied, if not quite jolly, undertaker with an Aloha shirt, Bronze and Silver Star citations, and a degree in cemetery management from Fort Sam Houston. As we move to the burial itself, however, the irony gives way to pathos.

With a style that exemplifies Hemingway's insistence on accurate description and understated emotion, Didion recalls the graveside ritual:

All I can tell you about the next ten minutes is that they seemed a very long time. We watched the coffin being carried to the grave and we watched the pallbearers lift the flag, trying to hold it taut in the warm trade wind. The wind was blowing hard, toppling the vases of gladioli set by the grave, obliterating some of the chaplain's words. . . . I was looking beyond the chaplain to a scattering of graves so fresh they had no headstones, just plastic markers stuck in the ground. "We tenderly commit this body to the ground," the chaplain said then. The men in the honor guard raised their rifles. Three shots cracked out. The bugler played taps. The pallbearers folded the flag until only the blue field and a few stars showed, and one of them stepped forward to present the flag to the father. (*WA* 142–43)

As the mourners begin to depart, "the father, transferring the flag from hand to hand as if it burned, said a few halting words to the pallbearers" (*WA* 143). Mr. Corley is careful to see that the grave is quickly covered because he does not like for families to return to the Mainland worrying whether their son is properly buried.

"We stood there a moment in the warm wind," Didion recalls, "then said goodbye. The pallbearers filed onto the Air Force bus. The bugler walked past, whistling 'Raindrops Keep Fallin' on My Head.' " Then

Didion concludes her piece with another specific observation followed by a shocking bit of general information that puts what she has witnessed in a broader perspective: "Just after four o'clock the father and mother came back and looked for a long while at the covered grave, then took a night flight back to the Mainland. Their son was one of 101 Americans killed that week in Vietnam" (*WA* 144).

In her 20 February 1970 *Life* column, "On the Last Frontier with VX and GB," Didion looks at some patriotic Americans who identify the national interest with the military policies of the federal government just as confidently as the supporters of the Vietnam War did. Here she writes of the government's intention to store a vast shipment of VX and GB nerve gas on 20,000 acres outside Hermiston, Oregon. The gas would be contained in regular mounds of "reinforced concrete covered with sod and sagebrush, 1,001 mounds rising from the earth in staggered rows and laced with fifty miles of rail track."[6] In her typically understated style, Didion concentrates less on the government's plans than on Hermiston's eager cooperation with those plans.

Still flush with the boom spirit of the frontier, the townspeople are certain that by storing the nerve gas in their community, and thus incidentally boosting the town's economy, they will be performing a patriotic service. We read, for example, of Joe Burns, "a mild-mannered funeral director who had helped draft a letter to President Nixon saying how much the citizens of Hermiston wanted the extra nerve gas." When queried about the possible safety hazards, Burns replies: "They talk about a few drops of it killing thousands of people. Well, really, you'd need pretty ideal conditions for that. And if you give yourself an injection within 30 seconds, there's no effect whatsoever." Not only do the good folks of Hermiston seem to share their undertaker's optimism, but they also believe that those who oppose the nerve gas are "from Portland and Eugene and somehow under the sway of . . . 'the academic-community-Moratorium-and-other-mothers-for-peace-or-whatever.' "

It took Didion a couple of days in Hermiston to realize that she "was not in a frontier town at all but in a post-frontier town, which was always a little different." What she was seeing in Hermiston was the sort of enthusiasm about industrial development and civilization in general that occurred all over the West "after the neurasthenics and the mystics had moved on" and the bride had come to Yellow Sky. (The fact that development and civilization are, in this case, represented by weapons of mass destruction may heighten the irony but does not alter the basic point.) "I was in a place," Didion writes, "where people felt, just as other settlers had felt in the waning days of other frontiers, somehow redeemed, cut free from the ambiguities of history."

The people of Hermiston, as Didion depicts them, seem like nothing so much as updated figures from a Sinclair Lewis novel, especially the old-timers in *Main Street*'s postfrontier Gopher Prairie. However, the author's attitude toward these people is neither contemptuous nor dismissive. Instead, it is more like the benign condescension an adult might show toward a child's innocence.[7] She tells us that these people "believed in 'growth,' in 'the future,' in 'doubling the population' as an unequivocal good." But Didion does not share their faith. "Where I come from in California," she says, "we have already seen the future and it does not work, but there was no way of telling anyone that on the last frontier."

Another group of last frontiersmen gathered at the Miramar Hotel in Santa Monica in the waning days of the sixties. The occasion was the national congress of the U. S. Junior Chamber of Commerce, "a relentless succession of keynote banquets and award luncheons and prayer breakfasts and outstanding-young-men forums" (*WA* 92). Didion does not rail against the Babbittry of these people nor does she describe them in such a way that they make fools of themselves. (The ironic distance is somewhat narrower than when she is writing about nerve gas in Hermiston, Oregon.) Instead, a part of her seems to identify with the peculiar homelessness—if not the specific values—of these fugitives from history. That they do not regard themselves as cultural anachronisms only makes their plight more poignant, the specific quality of despair—as Kierkegaard noted—being an unawareness that it is despair.

The essay concludes with Didion sitting in the Miramar lobby late one afternoon, listening to a couple of Jaycees discuss student unrest and the possibility that on-campus Jaycee groups might be the "solution" to this social problem. "I thought about this astonishing notion for a long time," Didion writes. "It occurred to me finally that I was listening to a true underground, to the voice of all those who have felt themselves not merely shocked but personally betrayed by recent history. It was supposed to have been their time. It was not" (*WA* 95). These people have the ability to live as if the sixties had never occurred. But Joan Didion knows, as they do not, that "1950 was more than 20 years ago."[8]

Chapter Five
Selling Somebody Out

"It is the great word of the twentieth century," writes Norman Mailer.
"If there is a single word our century has added to the potentiality of
language, it is ego."[1] The cult of personality in American life would
seem to substantiate Mailer's observation. Although this cult probably
began with the advent of motion pictures, it accelerated in the sixties
and seventies as the children of the postwar baby boom supplied a
natural market for the emerging media of television and rock music.

Originally centered in the world of entertainment, this cult is suffi-
ciently broad to encompass figures in such diverse fields as politics,
sports, and finance. As religious and community life have eroded and
the family structure itself has fragmented, Americans have focused
increasing reverence on exemplars of worldy fame, wealth, and beauty.
In the process, literature and the other traditional arts have been sup-
planted by popular culture. Whether the medium be celluloid, cathode
rays, or electrified dissonance, the message is the same: our celebrities
are our gods.

Public fascination with culture heroes has created in its wake a whole
genre of personality journalism. From Edward R. Murrow's "Person to
Person" television show in the fifties to *People* magazine in the seventies
and beyond, the broadcast and print media have sought to make our
heroes more accessible to us, or at least to give us the impression of
having done so. This effort has produced mixed results. At its worst
personality journalism can be tawdry, sensational, and numbingly dull;
but at its best it can suggest provocative social and philosophical insights.[2] In the personality sketches written by Joan Didion, these latter
qualities tend to prevail.

In the American Grain

In her *Slouching Towards Bethlehem* essay "7000 Romaine, Los Angeles
38," Didion writes about one of the most fascinating and enigmatic
folk heroes in recent American history, Howard Hughes. A public man

for much of his life, Hughes was a noted rake, a world-famous aviator, and—according to *Fortune*—"the proprietor of the largest pool of industrial wealth . . . under the absolute control of a single individual" (*STB* 69). He was also the romantic ideal of Joan Didion's youth.[3] Her essay, however, does not deal with the public Hughes. Just as he did not appear in public during the last years of his life, neither does he appear in "7000 Romaine." Instead of depicting the man himself, Didion presents us with "the folklore of Howard Hughes . . . , the way people react to him . . . , the terms they use when they talk about him" (*STB* 68). Her interest in the visible embodiments of the Hughes legend, she tells us, is similar to the fascination of Arthurian scholars with the Cornish coast.

7000 Romaine is a building owned by Hughes "in that part of Los Angeles familiar to admirers of Raymond Chandler and Dashiell Hammett: the underside of Hollywood, south of Sunset Boulevard, a middle-class slum of 'model studios' and warehouses and two-family bungalows" (*STB* 68). A locked building with an insincere "WELCOME" mat, 7000 Romaine is the "communications center" of the Hughes empire. Didion's essay, however, is not about this "communications center," nor ultimately about Hughes himself, so much as it is about the mythopoeic sense of the American people.

That we have made a hero out of Howard Hughes tells us that "the secret point of money and power in America is neither the things that money can buy nor power for power's sake . . . , but absolute personal freedom, mobility, privacy." What Didion couldn't know at the time she wrote this piece is that Hughes's passion for privacy would eventually dwarf his desire for personal freedom and mobility and render his power and money useless. In 1967 Didion could say that Hughes was "not merely antisocial but grandly, brilliantly, surpassingly, asocial . . . , the last private man, the dream we no longer admit" (*STB* 72). By the time he died, malnourished and intestate, a decade later, that dream of privacy had become a nightmare of isolation—the downside of insisting too strenuously on the right to be left alone.

A very different kind of western individualism is represented by the painter Georgia O'Keeffe. Didion recalls an afternoon she spent with Quintana viewing a huge O'Keeffe canvas at the Chicago Art Institute. When her daughter asked her "who drew" the *Sky Above Clouds* canvas, Didion told her, and Quintana replied, "I need to talk to her" (*WA* 126). Quintana was making, Didion observes, "an entirely unconscious but quite basic assumption about people and the work they do. She was assuming that the glory she saw in the work reflected a glory in its maker, that the painting was the painter. . . . *Style is character"* (*WA* 126–27).

What Didion sees as the peculiar quality of Georgia O'Keeffe's style and character is something that in the very old we call crustiness or eccentricity. O'Keeffe, according to Didion, "is simply hard, a straight shooter, a woman clean of received wisdom and open to what she sees" (*WA* 127). A child of the Wisconsin prairie, Georgia O'Keeffe grew up playing with china dolls and painting watercolors of cloudy skies because sunlight was too hard to do. She knew that she wanted to be an artist before she had even seen a picture that interested her, and, when she became displeased with the sort of art education she was getting as a young woman in New York, she headed back west—stopping first in Texas and later in New Mexico. She painted exactly as she pleased and eventually forced the art world to accept her on her own terms.

Didion concludes her essay by quoting Miss O'Keeffe's reminiscence of those years she spent in Texas. As she and her sister Claudia walk toward the horizon, watching the evening star come out, Georgia observes, "That evening star fascinated me. . . . It was in some way very exciting to me." Claudia has a gun, and, as the sisters walk, she throws bottles into the air and shoots them before they hit the ground. But Georgia has only the "walk into nowhere and the wide sunset space with the star." In a way Didion's "interest is compelled as much by the sister Claudia with the gun as by the painter Georgia with the star, but only the painter left us this shining record" (*WA* 130).

The shining record left by the subject of Didion's affectionate tribute "John Wayne: A Love Song" also compels her interest. In fact, John Wayne is so much a part of our collective national consciousness that Didion moves easily between the first-person-singular and the first-person-plural in describing her feelings about the Duke. Like Georgia O'Keeffe, John Wayne was an individual for whom character and style were one. And even more than Howard Hughes, he was for Didion a lifelong figure of romance. This "love song" is structured symmetrically, as it begins with a discussion of Didion's childhood infatuation with Wayne, proceeds to give us a camera-eye view in prose of the Duke filming his one hundred sixty-fifth movie, and concludes by describing a dinner engagement that includes Wayne, an adult Didion, and their respective spouses. Although this shifting focus is only partially effective—the middle of the essay is perhaps disproportionately long—Didion has found in John Wayne something she has lacked in certain of her other essays: a subject commensurate with her ability to write about it.

In a sense, though, the author's subject is less an actual man than it is the ongoing relationship between herself and a mythic presence on the motion picture screen, a relationship that began in the summer of 1943 when she was eight years old. At that time her father was stationed at Peterson Field in Colorado Springs, a place that Didion remembers primarily for a hot wind which brought dust from Kansas and for the artificial blue rain behind the bar at the Officer's Club. Under these circumstances her only refuge from boredom lay in "the darkened Quonset hut which served as a theater" (*STB* 29), where three or four afternoons a week she and her brother sat on folding chairs watching movies. "It was there," she writes, "that summer of 1943 while the hot wind blew outside, that I first saw John Wayne. Saw the walk, heard the voice. Heard him tell the girl in a picture called *War of the Wildcats* that he would build her a house, 'at the bend in the river where the cottonwoods grow' " (*STB* 29–30). The men whom Didion has known in the ensuing years have had many virtues, but none has been John Wayne, and none has taken her to the bend in the river where the cottonwoods grow. "Deep in that part of my heart where the artificial rain forever falls," she tells us, "that is still the line I wait to hear" (*STB* 30).

Didion's personal revelations take on added significance when one considers how many thousands, even millions, of Americans can say with her that John Wayne "determined forever the shape of certain of our dreams" (*STB* 30). It was for this reason that the news of Wayne's initial bout with lung cancer proved so traumatic. The Duke's illness was an impingement of reality upon that dream world where nothing bad could happen. Thus it was with a certain foreboding that the author went to Mexico to observe Wayne filming *The Sons of Katie Elder,* the picture that had been so long delayed by his illness. At this point Didion removes herself from the center of the essay and focuses instead upon the peculiarly male camaraderie of the movie set, involving Wayne, Dean Martin, and director Howard Hathaway—down there in Durango, Mexico. Apparently, the conclusion we are to draw is that the Duke had, in fact, "licked the big C" (only a temporary victory, as it turned out) and that he was still the molder of dreams. This latter fact is amply demonstrated when, at the end of her essay, Didion tells us of the dinner she and her husband shared with Wayne and his wife and of her efforts to lose "the sense that the face across the table was in certain ways more familiar than my husband's."

Toward the end of a pleasant but ordinary evening "something happened." The room suddenly "seemed suffused with the dream," Didion recalls, "and I could not think why. Three men appeared out of nowhere, playing guitars." Wayne ordered more wine ("Pouilly-Fuisse for the rest of the table . . . and some red Bordeaux for the Duke"), and the men with the guitars continued playing what Didion finally recognized as "The Red River Valley" and the theme from *The High and the Mighty*. "They did not quite get the beat right," she says, "but even now I can hear them, in another country and a long time later, even as I tell you this" (*STB* 41).

Against the Grain

We can infer from her admiration of Howard Hughes, Georgia O'Keeffe, and John Wayne that individualism ranks pretty high on Joan Didion's list of preferred virtues. Even at her most conventional she is her own woman, and most attempts to pigeonhole her miss the mark rather badly. That does not mean, however, that she is a thoroughgoing iconoclast; for, even if individualism and iconoclasm frequently overlap, they are not the same thing. This distinction is borne out quite clearly in her discussions of Joan Baez, Patricia Campbell Hearst, and Bishop James Pike. Each of these individuals achieved fame through an ostensible dissent from traditional American values; however, Didion sees in their lives representative and typical as well as unique characteristics. In those lives we can read parables of our time.

When Didion did her piece on Joan Baez (1966), the folk music craze was sweeping American campuses, and more than just the usual left-wing suspects were beginning to question the wisdom of American policy in Vietnam. For those reasons, Baez had moved from the fringes of the entertainment world to the dreamily idealistic center of the counterculture. Her categorical opposition to violence made her a pariah first to the American middle class (she and the black concert singer Marian Anderson were the only entertainers ever denied use of Washington, D. C.'s Constitution Hall by the lily-white, superpatriotic Daughters of the American Revolution) and eventually to the pro-Communist Left. (Her work on behalf of the Vietnamese boat people helped expose the "worker's paradise" ruled by Hanoi for the Asian gulag that it was.)

But the woman who is the focus of Didion's essay is not so much an international celebrity as a local nuisance whose Institute for the Study of Nonviolence has local homeowners in Monterey County up in arms.

At an instinctive level, Didion's sympathies tend to be more with Baez than with her bourgeois attackers. The singer's "most striking characteristic," according to Didion, is "her absolute directness, her absence of guile." Baez even reminds the author of "what used to be called a lady" (*STB* 44). In contrast, the folks who want to run Baez out of the county are a bunch of local Philistines, who claim that her operation violates the clause in the county zoning code "which prohibits land use 'detrimental to the peace, morals, or general welfare of Monterey County' " (*STB* 42).

When the county Board of Supervisors meet to consider complaints against Baez and her school, the worst horror stories they hear are about men in beards occasionally asking directions on how to get to the school and about Baez's own tendency to sit under the trees on her property. Then it is the defendant's turn to speak: " 'Everybody's talking about their forty- and fifty-thousand-dollar houses and their property values going down,' she drawled finally, keeping her clear voice low and gazing levelly at the supervisors. 'I'd just like to say one thing. I have more than one *hundred* thousand dollars invested in the Carmel Valley, and I'm interested in protecting my property too' " (*STB* 45).

Didion's personal respect for Baez and her obvious disdain for the small-mindedness of the singer's Monterey County neighbors does not, however, lead to an endorsement of Baez's school. Didion is simply too much of a political skeptic to be taken in by the ingenuous idealism of the place. That skepticism comes through clearest in her description of the school's students. They are, she tells us, "on the average very young, very earnest, and not very much in touch with the larger scene, less refugees from it then children who do not quite apprehend it." Their belief in the political efficacy of nonviolence, for example, is more than a little naive. "They discuss a proposal from Berkeley for an International Nonviolent Army: 'The idea is, we go to Vietnam and we go into these villages, and then if they burn them, we burn too' " (*STB* 49).

Although Didion does not explicitly compare Baez's school to the Garden of Eden, one comes away from her essay thinking of the Monterey County retreat as the moral equivalent of a germ-free environment. It is "a place where the sun shines and the ambiguities can be set aside a little while longer, a place where everyone can be warm and loving and share confidences" (*STB* 58). At the end of the day the students are reluctant about gathering up their belongings, "and by the time they are ready to leave Joan Baez is eating potato salad with her fingers from a bowl in the refrigerator, and everyone stays to share it, just a little while longer where it is warm" (*STB* 60).

By the early seventies the nonviolent utopianism of the New Left had largely given way to the sort of armed nihilism that was mistaken in some circles for a second American Revolution. Many commentators date this transformation from the afternoon in May 1970 when Ohio National Guardsmen killed four students during disturbances on the campus of Kent State University. Exactly three years and nine months after that watershed event, a band of urban guerrillas calling themselves the Symbionese Liberation Army abducted the granddaughter of newspaper tycoon William Randolph Hearst from her apartment near the campus of the University of California at Berkeley. Hearst was held captive for fifty-seven days as various ransom demands (mostly involving the distribution of free food in the Oakland ghetto) were made by the SLA and partially met by the captive's father, Randolph Hearst.

On the fifty-eighth day, Patricia Campbell Hearst joined her captors, adopted the revolutionary name of Tania, and went underground. Over the next sixteen-and-a-half months, she carried a submachine gun and participated in a series of bank robberies and other crimes, until she was captured by the FBI on 18 September 1975. After redefecting to the upper class and copping an insanity plea that not even her attorney F. Lee Bailey could get a jury to accept, Hearst was sent to a relatively posh penal institution from which she was released by an executive commutation from President Jimmy Carter. The strange odyssey of Patricia Hearst, chronicled in the 1982 autobiography, could be seen as a symbol of many things. Not surprisingly, Joan Didion—in what is ostensibly a review of that autobiography—sees it as a California story.

Never one to miss a telling juxtaposition, Didion recalls that on the same day that Randolph Hearst's attempted food give-away in West Oakland degenerated into looting and general chaos, former California Senator William Knowland, "the most prominent member of the family that had run Oakland for half a century, had taken the pistol he was said to carry as protection against terrorists, positioned himself on a bank of the Russian River, and blown off the top of his head." True, Didion concedes, "there was no actual correlation between William Knowland lying face down in the Russian River and turkey legs thrown through windows in West Oakland, but the paradigm was manifest, two Californias."[4]

In a sense Patricia Campbell Hearst is caught between the two Californias (to paraphrase Matthew Arnold, one dead and the other powerless to be born). What Didion seems to find fascinating about her is Hearst's ability to adapt to changing circumstances with the amoral pragmatism of her frontier ancestors. (While other reviewers complained that Patty Hearst left things out of her book and allowed certain questions to linger, Didion points out that the book is quite detailed about how to lace a bullet with cyanide or to make a pipe bomb.) This pragmatism is apparently to be preferred to the integrity of those radicals who see life as "a question of your self-respect or your ass," and who declare quite smugly that "if you choose your ass, you live with nothing." Whatever one may say of Patricia Campbell Hearst, she always put her ass above all else.

Didion concludes her discussion of Patty Hearst by recalling having read a piece on the SLA in a March 1977 issue of an upscale community paper called the *Bay Guardian*. When she got the paper out to reread that piece, she noticed for the first time a long and favorable report on a San Francisco minister who was said to be a great moral leader and was even compared to Cesar Chavez. This clergyman was responsible for a " 'mind-boggling' range of social service programs—food distribution, legal aid, drug rehabilitation, nursing homes, free Pap smears—as well as for a '27,000-acre agriculture station.' " Once again we have the telling juxtaposition, because "this agricultural station was in Guyana, and the minister of course was the Reverend Jim Jones, who eventually chose self-respect over his own and nine hundred other asses."[5]

If her view of Joan Baez and Patricia Hearst is tinged with at least partial admiration, Didion's opinion of the late Episcopal Bishop of California—James Albert Pike—is one of utter contempt. Whereas Baez may possess the aura of a guileless lady and Hearst remind the author of a resourceful frontier pragmatist, Pike is an unambiguous reflection of much that is self-indulgent and meretricious in contemporary American culture. In her *White Album* essay "James Pike, American," Didion takes the trendy prelate apart.

Pike was born in Oklahoma in 1913 and won first prize in the Better Babies Contest at the Oklahoma State Fair two years running. (" 'I thought you would like that,' " his mother told his biographers "almost sixty years later, 'He started out a winner' " [*WA* 53].) After the death of his father, Pike and his mother moved to California, where young James was raised a Roman Catholic. At the age of eighteen, however, he became an agnostic and remained one throughout his college years at UCLA. He later went east to attend Yale Law School and subsequently to work for the Securities and Exchange Commission in Washington. At that time he wrote to his mother, "Practically every churchgoer you meet in our level of society is Episcopalian, and an R. C. or a straight Protestant is as rare as hen's teeth" (*WA* 54).

When Didion contemplates this letter, she thinks of Pike as resembling certain characters in the works of F. Scott Fitzgerald. He is "Gatsby coming up against the East," or Tom Buchanan with his vast carelessness "(some 25 years later, in Santa Barbara, when the Bishop of California's mistress swallowed 55 sleeping pills, he appears to have moved her from his apartment into her own before calling an ambulance, and to have obscured certain evidence before she died)," or even "Dick Diver, who also started out a winner, and tried to embrace the essence of the American continent in Nicole as James Albert Pike would now try to embrace it in the Episcopal Church" (*WA* 54–55). Pike is, for Didion, the sort of literary character who sometimes emerges in real life (others she mentions in this regard are Howard Hughes and Whittaker Chambers), "a character so ambiguous and driven and revealing of his time and place that his gravestone in the Protestant Cemetery in Jaffa might well have read only JAMES PIKE, AMERICAN" (*WA* 53).

Although he was an indifferent scholar, Pike's celebrity status placed him in the forefront of the radical theology of the sixties. American culture was permeated at that time with a kind of secular millennialism, a desire—in Eric Voegelin's phrase—to "immanentize the eschaton." As a sort of corollary to this development, many theologians sought to make their faith less supernatural and more "relevant" to the nonreligious world (Pike's one notable departure from this rationalist trend was a naive belief in spiritualism after the apparent suicide of his son Jim, Jr.). These were years of demythologizing, when an entire "theological" movement would proclaim the "death of God." (While it is true that Pike didn't go quite *that* far, he spoke only of God, having "streamlined the Trinity, eliminating the Son and the Holy Ghost" [*WA* 51].)

In that era of supreme hubris, James Albert Pike always seemed to be leading the pack, carrying "his peace cross (he had put away his pectoral cross for the duration of the Vietnam war, which outlived him) through every charlatanic thicket in American life, from the Center for the Study of Democratic Institutions to the Aspen Institute for Humanistic Studies to Spiritual Frontiers, which was at the time the Ford Founda-

tion of the spirit racket" (*WA* 57). After resigning his position as
Bishop of California, following an inconclusive heresy trial in which his
fellow bishops proved that Auberon Waugh was right when he said
that no one from the Pope to Mao Tse-tung could be sure that he was
not an Anglican, Pike bad-mouthed his former church in the pages of
Look and turned full time to the lecture and talk show circuit.

Five years later, James Albert Pike and his third wife rented a Ford
Cortina from Avis and drove into the Jordanian desert with two bottles
of Coca-Cola, because they wanted to experience the wilderness as Jesus
had. Although the young Mrs. Pike returned from that trip alive, her
husband was not so lucky. His body was found five days later in a
canyon by the Dead Sea. When Pike's brother-in-law joined the search
party to find the man who had started out a winner, but who was
already lying dead in the desert, he prayed for the assistance of God,
Jim Jr., and Edgar Cayce. "I think," writes Didion, "I have never heard
a more poignant trinity" (*WA* 58).

Chapter Six
Some Places of the Mind

One of the most frequently assigned topics in introductory composition classes is to describe a place. It is assumed that such an assignment is simple because it does not require expository analysis, argumentative logic, or even narrative chronology—only a keen sense of observation. The problem is that such essays (when produced by inexperienced writers) generally lack both purpose and personality. Places, like the Sabbath, were made for man, not the other way around. Unlike most student writers, Joan Didion instinctively realizes this and thus sees the description of a place as another way of saying *I*. (An entire section of *Slouching Towards Bethlehem* is entitled "Seven Places of the Mind.") Didion would surely agree with Eudora Welty when she writes: "One place comprehended can make us understand other places better. Sense of place gives equilibrium; extended, it is sense of direction too. Carried off we might be in spirit, and should be, when we are reading or writing something good; but it is the sense of Place going with us still that is the ball of golden thread to carry us there and back and in every sense of the word to bring us home."[1]

Where No One Is

There are any number of bizarre places where Joan Didion can go when she wants to get away from it all. One such place—an abandoned and decaying fortress sitting off the coast of California—is the remnant of what used to be the federal prison at Alcatraz. "It is not an unpleasant place to be," Didion writes, "out there on Alcatraz with only the flowers and the wind and a bell buoy moaning and the tide surging through the Golden Gate, but to like a place like that you have to want a moat" (*STB* 205).

In her essay on Alacatraz Didion tells of the present state of the prison building and of the daily routine of the government employees who now guard this historic piece of federal property. (It ceased functioning as a prison in March 1963.) Ever the clear-eyed observer,

Didion gives us an interesting and seemingly objective report of what she sees. However, from beneath the surface and between the lines of that report, there emerges the image of a woman who—by her own admission—at times does want a moat. Significantly, that aspect of her psyche which is touched by Alcatraz is suggested by the title of her essay—"Rock of Ages." Didion has appropriated a line from the famous hymn by Augustus Toplady, a line which in context reads: "Rock of ages, cleft for me, let me hide myself in thee."[2] For Didion the rock of Alcatraz, not Toplady's rock of faith, comes to embody the allure of security and isolation.

The sense of timelessness that isolation breeds is reinforced by the prison itself: "The buildings seem quite literally abandoned. The key locks have been ripped from the cell doors and the big electrical locking mechanisms disconnected. The tear-gas vents in the cafeteria are empty and the paint is buckling everywhere, corroded by the sea air, peeling off in great scales of pale green and ocher" (STB 207). Didion tells us of standing in a cell next to a makeshift calendar, "the months penciled on the wall with the days scratched off, May, June, July, August of some unnumbered year" (STB 208).

There is also a pervasive irony in an abandoned prison. When Alcatraz was in operation, its full resources were devoted to keeping prisoners in; now that there are no more prisoners, the government is interested only in keeping intruders out. As a more or less authorized intruder, Didion tells us that she "tried to imagine the prison as it had been, with the big lights playing over the windows all night long and the guards patrolling the gun galleries and the silverware clattering into a bag as it was checked in after meals, tried dutifully to summon up some distaste, some night terror of the doors locking and the boat pulling away" (STB 208). But her imagination fails her, or perhaps it leads in other directions. She likes it there on Alcatraz, and, echoing fellow California native Robert Frost, she says of her return to the mainland, "I could tell you that I came back because I had promises to keep, but maybe it was because nobody asked me to stay" (STB 208).

Didion finds something of this same sense of womblike security at another western landmark—Hoover Dam. In her essay "At the Dam" she puts herself in touch with a natural element that is austerely indifferent to human concerns. Her preoccupation here is not with water in its original power and beauty, but as it is harnessed by the artifice of technology. In a sense the phenomenon she is describing is an idea as well as a physical reality. It is the "showpiece of the Boulder Canyon project, the several million tons of concrete that made the Southwest plausible, the fait accompli that was to convey, in the innocent time of its construction, the notion that mankind's brightest promise lay in American engineering" (*WA* 199).

Even if the dam can be seen as "a monument to a faith since misplaced" (*WA* 199), there is something strangely comforting about the engulfing power of the place. When the emotional pressure becomes too great for Maria Wyeth in *Play It as It Lays,* she goes out to Hoover Dam to be enraptured by the torrents surging around her: "She wanted to stay in the dam, lie on the great pipe itself, but reticence saved her from asking."[3] Perhaps what is at work here is a desire to transcend the mutable by losing oneself in the eternal, or at least in something more permanent than any of our mortal lives. It is a desire—and vanity—as old as the Tower of Babel.

Didion begins to recognize the force of this desire when she is shown a star map that fixes the date on which the dam was dedicated. She speaks to the Reclamation man who tells her that this map was "for when we were all gone and the dam was left" (*WA* 201). Although that statement made no impression on her at the time, Didion thought of it later that day, "with the wind whining and the sun dropping behind a mesa with the finality of a sunset in space." "Of course, that was the image I had seen always," she concludes, "seen it without quite realizing what I saw, a dynamo finally free of man, splendid at last in its absolute isolation, transmitting power and releasing water to a world where no one is" (*WA* 201).

A somewhat more conventional vacation spot is the setting of Didion's 1965 essay "Guaymas, Sonora." This short prose sketch follows the Dunnes as they leave a rainy Los Angeles, where a cliff is crumbling into the surf and getting dressed in the morning is a chore, to the more spartan environment of a desert town in Mexico. Much of the effect of this piece is due to its clear, supple, almost hypnotic prose. Like Hemingway, Didion eschews heavy subordination and relies instead on a loose, expansive sentence structure—simple clauses strung together with coordinating conjunctions. Slipping easily from the past to the present tense, she puts us into the automobile with her as she makes her trip south.

"After Nogales on Route 15," she writes, "there is nothing but the Sonoran desert, nothing but mesquite and rattlesnakes and the Sierra Madre floating to the east, no trace of human endeavor but an occasional Pemex truck hurtling north and once in a while in the distance the dusty Pullman cars of the Ferrocarril del Pacifico" (*STB* 214). Then, at the end of a week in Guaymas, during which John caught eight sharks and Joan read an oceanography textbook, the Dunnes decided they wanted to do something, "but all there was to do was visit the tracking station for an old space program or go see John Wayne and Claudia Cardinale in *Circus World*." It was then that they "knew it was time to go home" (*STB* 216).

What makes this more than just an elegantly written travel piece is Didion's insistence that there are some states of lethargy that can be cured only by travel to a desert. "We went to get away from ourselves," she writes, "and the way to do that is to drive down through Nogales some day when the pretty green places pall and all that will move the imagination is some place difficult, some desert" (*STB* 214). She tells us later that "the point is to become disoriented, shriven, by the heat and the deceptive perspectives and the oppressive sense of carrion" (*STB* 215). The religious, ascetic overtones of the word "shriven" suggest that what she and Dunne are seeking is nothing less than a ritual cleansing of the soul. For that process to be complete, however, they need to know when it is time to "go home," to reenter the everyday world they have fled. "The desert, any desert," Didion reminds us, "is indeed the valley of the shadow of death; come back from the desert and you feel like Alcestis reborn" (*STB* 214).

Cities of Man

With the essays "In Bogota," "Seacoast of Despair," and "Marrying Absurd," Didion is very much in the midst of what passes for civilization in the Western hemisphere during the latter third of the twentieth century. In the first of these sojourns she takes us close to the Equator, near the mythical republic of Boca Grande, to the Colombian capitol of Bogota. She tells us she had been on the coast, in Cartegena, until the allure of Bogota became irresistible. "In Bogota it would be cool," Didion writes. "In Bogota one could get the *New York Times* only two days late and the *Miama Herald* only one day late and also emeralds and bottled water. In Bogota there would be fresh roses in the bathrooms at the Hotel Tequendama and hot water twenty-four hours a day and numbers to be dialed for chicken sandwiches from room service" (*WA* 187).

Like much of South America, Bogota represents a mix of cultures— including various indigenous, North American, and European traditions. During her stay Didion came in contact with all three. When visiting the Gold Museum of the Banco de la Republica, for example, she thinks "of the nights when the Chibcha Indians lit bonfires on the Andes and confirmed their rulers at Guatavita" (*WA* 188–89). She quotes anthropologist Olivia Vlahos, who describes how the prospective ruler would step into the firelight, his naked body covered with resin. Priests would spread gold dust on the resin until the royal figure *"gleamed like a golden statue."* Then the monarch-to-be stepped onto a raft *"which was cut loose to drift into the middle of the lake. Suddenly he dived into the black water. When he emerged the gold was gone, washed clean from his body. And he was king"* (*WA* 189).

The influence of *norteamericana* (or U.S.) culture is a bit more immediate; though even here one can perceive a "slight but definite dislocation of time" (*WA* 190). (The movie theaters—in 1973—are showing U.S. films from the mid-sixties and "the English-language racks of paperback stands were packed with Edmund Wilson's *The Cold War and the Income Tax,* the 1964 Signet edition" [*WA* 190].) The Americans staying in Bogota convene at the U.S. embassy, and in their dealings with the native population they take elaborate pains to be inoffensive. For example, Didion tells us of an American actor who took cold showers for two weeks before realizing that the hot and cold taps in his room had been reversed. (One is reminded of a country girl from Sacramento shivering with a cold in an air-conditioned hotel room in New York.) "He had never asked, he said, because he did not want to be considered an arrogant *gringo*" (*WA* 192).

Our final image of Bogota is of Didion eating lunch in "the chilly dining room of the Hosteria del Libertador" after coming up from a cathedral built deep in a Colombian salt mine. ("One could think of Chibcha sacrifices here, of the conquistador priests struggling to superimpose the European mass on the screams of the slaughtered children"; but, since the cathedral was built by the Banco de la Republica in 1954, one would be wrong [*WA* 195–96].) She describes the ornate "battery of silverplated flatware and platters and *vinaigrette* sauceboats" and the equally grand contingent of waiters—"little boys, twelve or thirteen years old, dressed in tailcoats and white gloves and taught to serve as if this small inn on an Andean precipice were Vienna under the Hapsburgs" (*WA* 196). The author watches one of these young waiters in white gloves as he picks up an empty wine bottle, fits it precisely into a wine holder, and proceeds into the kitchen—marching stiffly, "glancing covertly at the *maitre d'hotel* for approval." Remembering this scene later, Didion concludes that she "had never before seen and would perhaps never again see the residuum of European custom so movingly and pointlessly observed" (*WA* 197).

The residuum of a very different kind of culture can be found in the Newport, Rhode Island, homes of some celebrated turn-of-the century robber barons. And it is to this different culture that Didion turns her attention in "Seacoast of Despair." What she sees in the homes of men such as Cornelius Vanderbilt is the old lesson that money doesn't bring happiness. What saves this insight from hopeless banality is Didion's realization that happiness was never the point for Vanderbilt and company. "Happiness is, after all, a consumption ethic," Didion notes, "and Newport is the monument of a society in which production was seen as the moral point, the reward if not exactly the end, of the economic process" (*STB* 210). What one finds in Newport is "a sense not of how prettily money can be spent but of how harshly money is made" (*STB* 211).

Although Newport is located on the Atlantic coast, Didion understands the social and economic forces at work here in terms of her own peculiarly West Coast sensibility. She notes, for example, that if Newport lacks the expansiveness of the West, it does possess a masculine stridency that is characteristic of the frontier. For this reason, she sees Newport as "closer in spirit to Virginia City than to New York, to Denver than to Boston" (*STB* 211). Ultimately, however, Newport lacks the characteristic that virtually defines the West for Didion—that romantic view of human possibilities one finds embodied in a California dream castle such as William Randolph Hearst's San Simeon. The homes of Newport seem, in contrast, almost a Calvinist homiletic in stone.

In making this quasi-theological argument, Didion writes, "It is hard for me to believe that Cornelius Vanderbilt did not sense, at some point in time, in some dim billiard room of his unconscious, that when he built 'The Breakers' he damned himself" (*STB* 212). That Vanderbilt would have been more likely to view his success as a matter of divine election, were he to give the matter any thought at all, seems not to have occurred to Didion. It is for the author of *Slouching Towards Bethlehem,* not the captains of industry, that conspicuous consumption resembles a camel trying to pass through the eye of a needle.

If Newport represents the denouement of the American dream—the triumph of memory over hope—then Las Vegas is the future realized, an ambience wrenched out of time and removed from the matrix of ordinary human desire. In commenting on this town, Didion writes: "I have never understood why the point . . . [of going there] is believed to be money, when the place is in fact profoundly immaterial, all symbol, all light and shadow and metaphor, a tableau vivant of lust and greed. I know Las Vegas to be a theater dedicated to the immediate gratification of every impulse, but I also know it to be a theater designed to numb those very impulses it promises to gratify."[4] Vegas is an oxymoronic city in which the distinctions between East and West, wilderness and civilization, and—indeed—illusion and reality are permanently blurred. Didion finds an ideal synecdoche for the surrealism of the place in the industry described in "Marrying Absurd."

Because Nevada has the most liberal marriage laws in the nation (no blood test and no waiting period before a license is issued), it is possible to get married on the spot in Las Vegas at almost any time of the day or night. In fact, between 9:00 P.M. and midnight on 26 August 1965, a record 171 couples plighted their respective troths in Las Vegas's assembly-line marriage parlors. (This otherwise unremarkable Thursday happened to be the last day that a man could improve his draft status simply by getting married.) Sixty-seven of these couples were united by a single justice of the peace, Mr. James A. Brennan. One of those weddings was performed at the Dunes and the other sixty-six in Mr. Brennan's office. " 'I got it down from five to three minutes,' Mr. Brennan said later of his feat. 'I could've married them *en masse,* but they're people, not cattle. People expect more when they get married' " (*STB* 80).

In "Marrying Absurd" the narrator virtually disappears. No autobiographical recollection personalizes the sketch, and no complex argument demands our assent. (This is in contrast to Dunne's *Vegas: A Memoir of a Dark Season,* a deeply personal book that finds in the tawdriness of Las Vegas an objective correlative for the inner turmoil its author was experiencing at the time.) What we have instead is a series of deadpan vignettes in which Didion's material judges itself. Consider, for example, our final glimpse of love on the neon desert. A wedding party consisting of the bride, her parents, and her new husband sits in a Strip restaurant. The bride still wears her gown, and her mother, a corsage. A bored waiter pours pink champagne—"on the house"—for everyone but the bride, who is too young to be served. " 'You'll need something with more kick in it than that,' the bride's father said with heavy jocularity to his new son-in-law; the ritual jokes about the wedding night had a certain Panglossian character, since the bride was clearly several months pregnant. Another round of pink champagne, this time not on the house, and the bride began to cry. 'It was just as nice,' she sobbed, 'as I hoped and dreamed it would be' " (*STB* 83).

As evocative and well crafted as these "place essays" may be, Didion seems to have written them from a distance. They lack the personal connection that identifies a geographic region as a writer's own literary property. That such a connection exists between particular places and particular writers is readily acknowledged by Didion in her affectionate tribute to James Jones, the man who made Honolulu come alive in his remarkable novel *From Here to Eternity*. "Certain places seem to exist," that tribute reads, "because someone has written about them. . . . A place belongs forever to whoever claims it hardest, remembers it most obsessively, wrenches it from itself, shapes it, renders it, loves it so radically that he remakes it in his image" (*STB* 146). By such reckoning, it is neither the isolated retreats nor the exotic resorts of her maturity but the lost homeland of her childhood that is Joan Didion's own little postage stamp of soil.

Chapter Seven

The Real Eldorado

According to Joan Didion, "it is characteristic of Californians to speak grandly of the past as if it had simultaneously begun, *tabula rasa,* and reached a happy ending on the day the wagons started west. . . . California is a place in which a boom mentality and a sense of Chekhovian loss meet in uneasy suspension; in which the mind is troubled by some buried but ineradicable suspicion that things had better work here, because here, beneath that immense bleached sky, is where we run out of continent" (*STB* 172). If Didion's own writings about California contain more Chekhovian loss than boundless optimism, it is because the situation we face today is radically different from that which confronted the early settlers.

As a people we moved west and conquered the wilderness, but now the journey is over. Rather than finding a new Eden in the West, many people have come to feel only depression and a sense of betrayal. In John Steinbeck's "The Leader of the People," for example, we read of an old man who once led a wagon train across the continent to California. Now he lives next to the ocean telling bored listeners about his bygone adventures. His daughter says of the journey, "That was the big thing in my father's life. . . . It was a big thing to do, but it didn't last long enough."[1] This old man is the sort of pathetic and anachronistic hero Didion would understand. He tells his grandson Jody, "There's a line of old men along the shore hating the ocean because it stopped them."[2]

Fire and Rain

In his study of the modern American novel, *Bright Book of Life,* Alfred Kazin points out that Didion "describes southern California in terms of rattlesnakes, cave-ins, earthquakes . . . , and the terrible wind called the Santa Ana."[3] (If Sacramento is the Eden from which she has been exiled by the exigencies of history, perhaps Los Angeles is the Gomorrah in which that same history has condemned her to live.) This elemental understanding of place is probably best reflected in her essays "Los Angeles Notebook," "Quiet Days at Malibu," and "Holy Water."

In the first of these Didion describes the sense of foreboding Southern Californians feel prior to the onslaught of a Santa Ana wind: "The baby frets. The maid sulks. I rekindle a waning argument with the telephone company, then cut my losses and lie down, given over to whatever it is in the air. To live with the Santa Ana is to accept, consciously or unconsciously, a deeply mechanistic view of human behavior" (STB 217).

The extreme aridity of Los Angeles during the time of year known as the "fire season," when coupled with the fierceness of the Santa Ana wind, makes brush fires a not uncommon occurrence there. Perhaps for this reason, Didion is convinced that "the city burning is Los Angeles's deepest image of itself" (STB 220). (When the artist who is protagonist of Nathanael West's The Day of the Locust begins his final painting before apparently going insane, it is of the city burning. And when the Watts riots erupted a quarter century later, a driver on the Harbor Freeway would actually see the city on fire.) "Los Angeles weather is the weather of catastrophe, of apocalypse," Didion writes. ". . . The violence and the unpredictability of the Santa Ana affect the entire quality of life in Los Angeles, accentuate its impermanence, its unreliability. The wind shows us how close to the edge we are" (STB 220–21).

In 1978 a brush fire caught in Agoura, in the San Fernando Valley, and quickly spread across 25,000 acres and thirteen miles to the coast. There it jumped the Pacific Coast Highway—principal residential street of Malibu—and became "a half-mile fire storm generating winds of 100 miles per hour and temperatures up to 2500 degrees Fahrenheit." Didion tells us that "refugees huddled on Zuma Beach. Horses caught fire and were shot on the beach, birds exploded in the air. Houses did not explode but imploded, as in a nuclear strike" (WA 223). In all, the fire destroyed 197 houses, many of which belonged to or had belonged to people Didion knew. She tells of visiting a local orchid grower, Amado Vazquez, and finding his greenhouse in ruins: "The place was now a range not of orchids but of shattered glass and melted metal and the imploded shards of . . . thousands of chemical beakers." After bidding Amado Vazquez good-bye, she went with her husband and daughter "to look at the house on the Pacific Coast Highway in which we had lived for seven years. The fire had come to within 125 feet of the property, then stopped or turned or been beaten back, it was hard to tell which" (WA 223). In any case, the house was no longer theirs.

Having written movingly about the soil and traumatically about the wind and fire of California, Didion appropriately turns her attention to the remaining primal element—water. Because that element is essentially life-giving, the tone of "Holy Water" is more lyrical than apocalyptic. "The West begins where the average annual rainfall drops below twenty inches," writes Bernard DeVoto. To Joan Didion's mind, "this is maybe the best definition of the West I have ever read" (*WA* 65).

The specific occasion for her writing this essay was Didion's trip to the Operation Control Center of the California State Water project. Its main undertaking on the day of her visit was the draining of Quail, a Los Angeles County reservoir which has a capacity of 1,636,018,000 gallons. At that moment Didion claims to have known that the only vocation for which she had any instinctive affinity was to drain Quail herself. (She remembers being caught, at age seventeen, in a military surplus life raft in the construction of the Nimbus Afterbay Dam on the American River near Sacramento, trying to open a tin of anchovies with capers as the raft spun "into the narrow chute through which the river had been temporarily diverted," and "being deliriously happy" [*WA* 60].)

Later she tells of a poem by Karl Shapiro that she had torn from a magazine and pinned to her kitchen wall. Although the fragment of paper is now on the wall of a sixth kitchen and crumbles whenever she touches it, the last stanza has for Didion "the power of a prayer":

> *It is raining in California, a straight rain*
> *Cleaning the heavy oranges on the bough*
> *Filling the gardens till the gardens flow*
> *Shining the olives, tiling the gleaming tile*
> *Waxing the dark camellia leaves more green*
> *Flooding the daylong valleys like the Nile.*
>
> (*WA* 65)

Admitting that she had no further business at the reservoir, Didion says that she nevertheless "wanted to be the one, that day, who was shining the olives, filling the gardens and flooding the daylong valleys like the Nile. I want it still" (*WA* 66).

Didion's image of modern California, like Nathanael West's, has often been characterized as a portrait of a wasteland. (Certainly, Los Angeles in flames bears some symbolic affinity to the Unreal City of T. S. Eliot and Charles Baudelaire.) However, the flowing of water carries with it the possibility of growth and fertility. (It can also symbolize power and be the focus of a struggle for power, as in Roman Polanski's film *Chinatown*.) But like fire, it can also be both a cleansing and a purging element. That it is sometimes so for Joan Didion is suggested in a passage from her essay "On Morality." Here she says that if she were to follow her conscience, it would lead her out onto the desert where Marion Faye stood in *The Deer Park* praying, "as if for rain," that the fiery apocalypse would come from Los Alamos *"and clear the rot and the stench and the stink . . . {until} the world stands clear in the white dead dawn"* (*STB* 161).

Goldengrove Unleaving

Anyone wishing to understand Didion as a writer and moralist must sooner or later come to terms with her sense of identity as a daughter of the pre-Sunbelt American West. "In the middle of my life," she wrote in 1976, "it occurs to me that I think differently because I come from the coast."[4] A few years earlier Alfred Kazin had made much the same point when he wrote of Didion, "the story between the lines of *Slouching Towards Bethlehem* is surely not so much 'California' as it is her ability to make us share her passionate sense of it."[5] Nevertheless, Didion is no purveyor of facile nostalgia. She is never so lyrical about the California of her youth as to lose sight of its shortcomings nor so pessimistic about our present condition as to indulge a sentimental nihilism. The pervasive tone of her prose, even at its most elegiac, is one of irony. In a way Didion is to the upper-middle class of the Central Valley what Faulkner was to the Sartorises and Compsons of Mississippi—a chronicler of social change. The difference is that she has addressed the issue more personally than Faulkner in autobiographical essays that feature herself as the victim of that change. The supreme example of this is her memoir "Notes from a Native Daughter."

Twice during this essay Didion cites a regionalist catechism she learned as a girl in Sunday School:

> Q.   *In what way does the Holy Land resemble the Sacramento Valley?*
>
> A.   *In the type and diversity of its agricultural products.* (*STB* 174, 181)

(That it is the Sacramento Valley that resembles the Holy Land rather than the other way around may suggest the superiority of the new Eden to the old.) Striking the same note elsewhere in her essay Didion writes, "In at least one respect California . . . resembles Eden: it is assumed that those who absent themselves from its blessings have been banished, exiled by some perversity of heart. Did not the Donner-Reed Party, after all, eat its own dead to reach Sacramento?" (*STB* 176). What comes across most forcefully here is not so much the equation of California with the earthly paradise (a rather conventional notion, to be sure), but rather Didion's recognition that that paradise was an imaginary garden with real snakes in it.

Taken on its own terms, the Sacramento Didion describes seems a fairly pedestrian place. But the point of nostalgia is not that one's past was actually a golden age but that the alchemy of memory can make it so. When Didion remembers the California legislature in action, she remembers Saint Patrick's Day 1948 and red-faced assemblymen in green hats reading Pat-and-Mike jokes into the record or being entertained by the emissaries of a legendary lobbyist on the veranda of the Senator Hotel. The small-town garishness of this scene contrasts markedly with the sterile Sunbelt atmosphere in which the modern legislature operates. The veranda at the Senator Hotel has now been turned into an airline ticket office, "and in any case the legislature has largely deserted the Senator for the flashy motels north of town, where the tiki torches flame and the steam rises off the heated swimming pools in the cold Valley night" (*STB* 177).

"Notes from a Native Daughter" concludes with a scene that could have come right out of *Absalom, Absalom!*. Didion calls it "a Sacramento story." It is about a rancher who once lived outside of town on a spread of six or seven thousand acres. His one daughter went abroad and married a title, whom she brought home to live on the ranch. Her father then built them a large house, consisting of music rooms, conservatories, and a ballroom. Pretty soon they started giving "house parties that lasted for weeks and involved special trains." These people are now long dead, but an old man—the son of the rancher's daughter and her title—still lives on the place. That in itself is unremarkable, except that he does not live in the house: it burned over the years, room by room and wing by wing. Now "only the chimneys of the great house are still standing, and its heir lives in their shadow, lives by himself on the charred site, in a house trailer" (*STB* 185). Like a camera slowly panning backward, the structure of that last sentence reveals first the chimneys, then the charred site, and finally the house trailer. The syntax, as well as the content, tells a dramatic story of the passing of an old order.

What makes this "Sacramento story" distinctively western, as opposed to a transplanted bit of Southern Gothic, comes at the end of the next paragraph after Didion tells us that this is a story of her generation, one that will mean nothing to the children of the aerospace engineers. "They will have lost the real past," she says, "and gained a manufactured one, and there will be no way for them to know, no way at all, why a house trailer should stand alone on seven thousand acres outside town" (*STB* 186). It is those seven thousand acres, which we see now that the camera is back all the way, that is the authentic western note in this story.

One might protest that the rising generation can regain the real past simply by reading Didion, but the native daughter refuses to allow herself even that hint of self congratulation. If her "real past" is not manufactured, it may well be embroidered with liberal doses of cracked crab and August snow. She is even willing to admit the possibility, in her last paragraph, that "this has been a story not about Sacramento at all, but about the things we lose and the promises we break as we grow older" (*STB* 186). Change the first person plural to singular, and you have the essence of Joan Didion's California.

Kingdom of the Mad: "Sunset" and *Run River*

Although it is anyone's guess as to when Joan Didion began to realize that the Northern California she knew as a child was being transformed into what is now known as the Sunbelt, her first literary treatment of that theme came in a story called "Sunset," which she wrote as an undergraduate at Berkeley. Published in the spring 1956 issue of the student literary magazine *Occident,* this story tells of a young woman who experiences the difficulty of returning to an italicized sense of home when the italics are gone. A remarkably evocative bit of juvenalia, "Sunset" serves as an excellent introduction to Didion's later elegiac writing, especially to her first novel, *Run River* (1963).

The focal character of "Sunset" is Laura Cavanaugh Gannon, a native Californian who had moved to New York with her mother following her father's death. Laura is now married to Charlie Gannon, a well-meaning but insensitive businessman from Chicago who is considerably older than she. As the story opens, Charlie and Laura are driving to the graveyard where her father is buried. (Although the location is never specified, Didion's descriptions leave little doubt that the setting is the

Sacramento Valley.) Laura is clearly disturbed by the changes that have taken place since last she was home:

Nothing was the same after twelve years; she could not go back. All the land had been sold and subdivided (by dreaming men like Charlie, men with their eyes on the main chance), and even the house in which she had lived her first sixteen years had been turned into a day nursery—Barbara Murray (but her name was St. John, now) sent her children there, and had said that they were using Laura's wildflower and organdy bedroom as a finger-painting gallery. She could visit Barbara and the others now and they could talk of the same things, but there was always the barrier, strong as steel, of time and other worlds.[6]

Among those other worlds is the one to which Charlie Gannon belongs. Although he lives in Chicago and travels to the Coast only on business, he is the prototype of the New West carpetbagger—a figure more fully realized in *Run River*'s Ryder Channing. (As they are driving to the graveyard Laura reflects that "if Charlie were developing this land he would promote it as suburban upper-middle potential, and restrict it. 'In the California Manner,' he would say. 'Casual Country Living.' And he would call it 'River Oaks,' and keep the promotion subdued."[7] In essence, Charlie functions as a sociological symbol and, unfortunately, as little else. A weakly drawn character, he possesses neither the charm nor the menace of Didion's later, more vital, male characters.

Although we do not know the source of Laura's original attraction to Charlie, his age may have had something to do with it. Since she has had a very close relationship with her father (and a very strained one with her mother), it could be that in Charlie she hopes to find a substitute father. This desire, however, creates intolerable contradictions when Charlie accompanies Laura on the pilgrimage to her actual father's grave. When her husband attempts to console her, Laura lashes out, "Perhaps you should have married my mother."[8] (I suspect that Laura probably wishes she *could* trade husbands with her mother. Although no overtly incestuous feelings are suggested here, it is clear that Laura's bond with her father was stronger than any she is likely to forge with Charlie.) If it is the memory of her father that accounts in large part for Laura's sense of identity with her childhood home, his death— more than the superficial changes she has noted—may help to explain her present sense of homelessness. And her marriage to Charlie—the inadequate substitute father from the East—is simply the most immediate reminder of her alienation.

At one point she tries vainly to tell Charlie what it is she has lost. "It was always lovely on the river," she says. "Everything hung in a kind of fluid suspension. No time ever." When her husband insists that "you can't just want suspension," Laura replies, "It's all that counts"; and when he says in desperation, "Everything can belong to us," she responds epigrammatically, "Everything can belong to us. . . . But we don't belong to anything."[9] That lament, sounded at an early age, echoes throughout Joan Didion's writings about modern California.

Run River tells of the twenty-year marriage of Everett and Lily Knight McClellan. Both children of prosperous Sacramento Valley ranchers, Everett and Lily begin their life together by eloping to Reno. However, shortly after their wedding and the birth of their two children, the couple are separated as Everett goes off to the service during World War II. Feeling lonely and betrayed, Lily has an affair with a neighboring rancher and conceives his child. When Everett comes home from the war, having been given a hardship discharge because of the death of his father, he is unable to cope with his wife's confessions of infidelity. Lily then slips away to San Francisco to have an abortion. And in the remaining years of their marriage, she and Everett live lives of mutual recrimination.

As the McClellans' marriage disintegrates, the novel's focus widens to include the relationship of Everett's sister Martha with a charming young social climber named Ryder Channing. After five years of enjoying steady company and frequent sexual intimacies with Martha, Ryder abruptly marries a young socialite—Miss Bugsy Dupree. Unable to put her life back together, Martha takes a boat out one stormy night and drowns. At Everett's insistence she is buried on the ranch.

As the years go by Everett and Lily grow further apart, and Lily herself takes up with Ryder Channing. When the novel opens Ryder, who has been awaiting an assignation with Lily on the levee of the McClellan ranch, is shot by Everett. We are then afforded a retrospective view of the preceding two decades, 1938–59. When we return to time present, Everett and Lily are anticipating the arrival of the sheriff. Lily remains in the house as Everett returns to the murder scene. A second shot is heard, and we, along with Lily, realize that Everett McClellan has taken his own life. The beginning and end of Didion's novel have the makings of tabloid melodrama ("IRATE HUSBAND

SHOOTS RIVAL, SELF"). However, in the intervening chapters, we have seen a picture of personal and cultural disintegration of sufficient complexity to raise melodrama to the level of something resembling tragedy.

One of the most immediately striking features of *Run River* is a regionalism similar to what one finds in the literature of the Southern Renascence. A couple of years before the publication of *Run River*, Didion herself wrote that "the tension central to both the Southern and the Western experience is . . . [the] inability to distinguish between myth and reality."[10] She has also said that when she lived in New York she was "most comfortable in the company of Southerners. They seemed to be in New York as I was, on some indefinitely extended leave from wherever they belonged . . . , temporary exiles who always knew when the flights left for New Orleans or Memphis or Richmond or, in my case, California" (*STB* 230).

In certain key respects the California of 1946 resembles the Mississippi of 1866. In each case the end of a war brought the end of an era. The main difference is that the South was reconstructed by the heavy hand of carpetbaggers, while the social landscape of California was transformed by the more insidious but no less radical influence of real estate speculators and aerospace engineers. It is therefore a master stroke of irony that Ryder Channing, the character who most exemplifies the New West, should be a native of Tennessee.

One suspects, however, that if he had stayed home Channing would just as easily have exemplified the New South. (Although he possessees the ruthlessness of Margaret Mitchell's Rhett Butler, he is without Rhett's roguish sense of honor; all that Channing has to recommend him is a superficial social grace and a Dionysian sexual vigor.) Shortly after his marriage to the debutante Bugsy Dupree, Ryder joins her family's construction business and superintends a suburban housing development called Riverside City. When a prospective Riverside City couple from Chicago inquires about the appearance of a plastic lining at the bottom of Riverside Lake, Channing reassures them: "*You can relax. The lining will be covered with six inches of earth, so unless you come out to inspect it now, you'll never see it*" (*R* 219).

In one sense Channing is a predator who represents the wave of a future that Didion abhors. However, because he is himself a failure, he is victim as well as victimizer. He may have indirectly brought about the deaths of both Martha and Everett McClellan, but he precipitates his own destruction as well. Had his story been the focus of *Run River*, the novel would have been a lament for the frustrated dreamer who is unable to realize his aspirations or even attain a measure of self-knowledge. Ryder Channing is a man who learns only the literal and not the symbolic truth of Didion's epigraph from *Peck's 1837 New Guide to the West:* "The real Eldorado is still further on."

But it is not new arrivals such as Ryder Channing who are Didion's prime concern. The West functions in this novel less as a far-off Eldorado that will never be reached than as a home that will never be the same again. Some, like Everett McClellan's sister Sarah, abandon that home by making the Gatsby-like journey east. But Sarah is so peripheral as to be invisible. Didion's story is really of the longtime residents of Eden who have stayed to see the Garden go to seed around them. Or to put the matter more precisely, it is of the children of these longtime residents, young people who were brought up to a certain way of life that no longer exists. Those of the older generation either die out before the Fall is complete or, as in the case of Lily's mother, Edith Knight, adjust by selling off their land and spending their days watching the Dodgers on television. (This team of transplanted Easterners, who migrated from Brooklyn to Chavez Ravine as part of a real estate deal, is the New West writ large.) The young adults of the postwar era are Didion's lost generation. [12]

If Ryder Channing is an anemic Rhett Butler, Everett McClellan is a cut-rate Ashley Wilkes. With both his parents dead and one sister expatriated to the East, Everett has only his remaining sister, Martha; his wife, Lily; and his two children to give him a sense of identity and belonging. But after the death of Martha, the collapse of his marriage, and the rebellion of his children, he is left with nothing. He has long ago lost even the self-confidence needed to maintain the amenities of the past. It had always been his father's custom to invite the foreman and his wife to the house on the night the hop picking was finished. But Everett's foreman, Henry Sears, departs for town before Everett can invite him, and Everett does not even know what he could have said to Sears had he invited him. People had always responded instinctively to Everett's father: "He would have known, as Everett did not know, how to talk to Henry Sears" (*R* 150).

In many ways the most vivid and attractive character of the younger generation is Everett's sister Martha. She possesses wit, charm, and character—everything except the ability to survive in changing times. Her very reality is defined by her sense of belonging to a place and a tradition. It is only fitting that her destruction be due at least in part to the rapacity of a carpetbagger and that she be buried on the ranch in the shade of a Chekhovian cherry tree. She alone of the younger generation would have known how to talk to Henry Sears.

Martha's deeply rooted sense of tradition is apparent when she and Lily see Everett off at the train depot prior to his departure for the army. When Martha gives her brother a going-away gift, it is *The McClellan Journal: An Account of an Overland Journey to California in the Year 1848*. This reminds Lily of her surprise when as a child she had discovered that Martha's bedroom walls were not covered with Degas ballet dancers or scenes from *Alice in Wonderland* "but a framed deed signed by John Sutter in 1847, a matted list of the provisions carried on an obscure crossing in 1852, a detailed relief map of the Humboldt Sink, and a large lithograph of Donner Pass on which Martha had printed, in two neat columns, the names of the casualties and the survivors of the Donner-Reed crossing" (*R* 100).

Although Martha's drowning has an impact on all of the novel's major characters, Everett is the one most deeply affected. His relationship with his sister had been unusually close, as he and Martha seemed to reinforce each other's sense of identity. While Didion gives us no evidence of an overtly incestuous relationship, there is clearly a kind of spiritual marriage between brother and sister. (" 'You might marry Everett,' Martha McClellan had suggested to Lily, once when they were both children, 'if I decide not to' " [*R* 48].) When Everett kills Ryder Channing, it is ostensibly because Channing has cuckolded him. However, beneath the surface of this ostensible motivation, there is probably the exacerbating memory of Ryder's earlier violation of Martha. (After all, others in the Valley have bedded Lily with impunity.) If the dream of brother-sister incest is often part of the Edenic fantasy, [13] the end of that dream is one of the consequences of the Fall. In a sense Ryder Channing is the serpent in the Garden.

Of course, in addition to his very tangible transgressions, Channing is also the prime symbol of all the forces that have conspired to wreck the way of life the McClellans have known and loved. And by the time Didion's novel comes to an end, Everett can see evidences of this phenomenon everywhere, not least of all in the behavior and attitudes of his own children. If Everett is not the man his father was, his son, Knight, doesn't even aspire to be. At one point Knight sneeringly compares what is happening in the Valley to "something out of *The Cherry Orchard*" (*R* 248). Then, a few pages later, he probably seals Ryder Channing's doom by challenging his father's very manhood.

"*Last Saturday night,*" the boy snarls, "your wife was shacked up at Lake Tahoe. . . . They call her Lily Knight, not McClellan, *Knight*. Like she was never married at all. *So I guess you didn't count for much*" (R 253).

As one might infer from the foregoing, Lily does not have particularly close ties with the next generation, either. Having aborted one child, she discovers that her two remaining offspring are lost to her as well. Not only is Knight openly contemptuous of his family and its values, but her daughter, Julie, is well on her way to becoming a local tramp. In the last scene in which we see her with one of her children, Lily sits by Julie's bed listening to her even breathing, "unable to explain to Julie, any more than she could explain to herself, just where the trouble had begun" (R 254). When the highway patrol arrives to investigate the carnage on the dock, where Everett has killed both Ryder Channing and himself, Lily brushes the leaves from the arm she had held around Everett's corpse[14] and begins to "wonder what she would say . . . to Knight and to Julie" (R 264).

In the face of traumatic cultural change, Lily would seem to have had a greater need than ever for her husband's love. Instead, she became not so much an adultress as a loner. Even if Ryder Channing had never existed, one senses that the chasm between her and Everett would still have been unbridgeable. The reason may be that, like Laura Cavanaugh Gannon in "Sunset," Lily's strongest familial bond was not to a living husband but to a dead father (her being an only child rules out the kind of sibling ties that existed between Everett and Martha). Hearing of Walter Knight's fatal automobile accident, Lily says, "*I'm not myself if my father's dead*" (R 78), and remembers his giving her a childhood tour of the family graveyard. "I think nobody owns land," he had said, "until their dead are in it" (R 84).[15] Lily's sense of rootedness was defined largely in terms of her relationship with her father. When that was gone, so too was her link with anything outside herself.

Although Joan Didion has not written a novel that is—in a narrow and provincial sense—*about* California, *Run River* belongs to a particular time and place as surely as the writings of William Faulkner and Tennessee Williams do. If California is the place where a geographical eschatology leads to a sense of disillusionment and loss, then the social fragmentation depicted in *Run River* is appropriate to a California setting. As if to emphasize this point, Didion includes some observations about the journey west at the climax of her novel—just as we thought that the focus had been narrowed to the domestic ills of the McClellan family. Sitting in her needlepoint chair, virtually anticipating Everett's suicide, Lily sees her troubles and those of her family as part of a historical continuum that reaches back to frontier days:

She, her mother, Everett, Martha, the whole family gallery; they carried the same blood, come down through twelve generations of circuit riders, county sheriffs, Indian fighters, country lawyers, Bible readers, one obscure United States Senator from a frontier state a long time ago; two hundred years of clearings in Virginia and Kentucky and Tennessee and then the break, the void into which they gave their rosewood chests, their silver brushes; the cutting clean which was to have redeemed them all. They had been a particular kind of people, their particular virtues called up by a particular situation, their particular flaws waiting there through all those years, unperceived, unsuspected, glimpsed only cloudily by one or two in each generation, by a wife whose bewildered eyes wanted to look not upon Eldorado but upon her mother's dogwood. . . . What is it you want, she had asked Everett tonight. It was a question she might have asked them all. (*R* 262–63)

Everett and Martha McClellan have aspired to a kind of tragic heroism, only to find the sort of melodramatic death that creates more problems than it solves for those who are left behind. Lily, however, survives with a stoic resignation and a renewed commitment to the distinctly unpromising role of mother. In her meditation on the westward movement, she has come to realize the folly of seeking an Eldorado that will always be further on. What is finally enobling about the western heritage, Didion seems to be saying, is not the dream that gave it birth but the life force that enables some to survive the end of that dream. While Everett and Martha (and in his own way Ryder Channing too) have found an uneasy rest, Lily must drag herself home alive, once more to face the kingdom of the mad. [16]

Chapter Eight
The World in a Window

The year 1964 was crucial in Joan Didion's literary career. Having just published her first novel, *Run River,* she was afraid that she might never write another. "I sat in front of my typewriter," she tells us, "and believed that another subject would never present itself. I believed that I would be forever dry. I believed that I would 'forget how.' Accordingly, as a kind of desperate finger exercise, I tried writing stories" (*TS* 10). She wrote three stories that year and, except for classroom exercises while an undergraduate at Berkeley, none in any other year. In 1978 she collected those three stories—"Coming Home," "The Welfare Island Ferry," and "When Did Music Come This Way? Children Dear, Was It Yesterday?"—along with an introductory essay in the limited-edition volume *Telling Stories.*

Training with the Rockettes

Didion begins her introductory essay by recalling the traumatic experience of being in Mark Schorer's creative writing workshop in the fall of 1954 when all of her classmates seemed so much older and wiser than she. For ten years thereafter, she did not write another story, which is not to say that she stopped writing altogether. On the contrary, she was writing almost constantly—not just magazine articles and a first novel, but also merchandising and promotion copy for *Vogue.* It was in the process of writing captions designed to achieve a particular effect in a specified number of lines and with a predetermined number of characters that Didion "learned a kind of ease with words . . . , a way of regarding words not as mirrors of my own inadequacy but as tools, toys, weapons to be deployed strategically on a page." She learned that "less was more, smooth was better, and absolute precision essential to the monthly grand illusion." For Joan Didion, "going to work for *Vogue* was, in the late nineteen-fifties, not unlike training with the Rockettes" (*TS* 5).

If there is some question as to whether Didion is a better novelist or journalist, no one has yet made the case that her truest vocation is as a writer of short fiction—least of all Didion herself. In her introductory essay to *Telling Stories,* Didion points out the specific shortcomings of her three stories and argues that she has "no feel for the particular rhythms of short fiction, no ability to focus the world in the window" (*TS* 10). Her stories are unsuccessful as stories, she concedes, because her narrative impulse is not toward the small epiphany. Her imagination needs the range and scope afforded by the novel. Thus, when her stories most engage our interest, it is as extended notations toward an unwritten novel.

Judged in those terms, the most interesting of her three stories is also the one Didion had most difficulty placing. "Coming Home" appeared in the 11 July 1964 issue of the *Saturday Evening Post* and "The Welfare Island Ferry" in the June 1965 issue of *Harper's Bazaar,* but "When Did Music Come This Way?" was rejected by a number of commercial magazines and several literary reviews before finding a home in the Winter 1967 issue of the *Denver Quarterly*. The story was originally commissioned by Rust Hills, then fiction editor of the *Saturday Evening Post,* for a special theme issue on children. Quite a few writers were contacted, and all were guaranteed a minimum payment of $250 whether or not their stories were accepted. Didion was one of those who received that $250 "kill fee."

For the next two years the William Morris agency tried to sell Didion's story. A sample of the twenty-two rejection letters she received includes this comment from *Good Housekeeping:* "marvelously written, very real, and so utterly depressing that I'm going to sit under a cloud of angst and gloom all afternoon. . . . I'm sorry we are seldom inclined to give our readers this bad a time"; and this one from the *Atlantic Monthly:* "I hope you'll be sending us more of Joan Didion's work, but this didn't make it, so back to you" (*TS* 13). When the story was finally accepted by the *Denver Quarterly,* Didion was paid the princely sum of $50, or one-fifth of what the *Post* had given her for refusing to use it.

Although "When Did Music Come This Way?" will probably never be included in an anthology of great American short stories, it is nevertheless Didion's finest effort in that genre and one that proved an indispensable exercise in the development of her fictive technique. It was in this story, she tells us, "that I taught myself—or began to teach myself—how to make narrative tension out of nothing more than the juxtaposition of past and present." She says she wishes that she had "known what I learned in this story before I ever wrote my first novel. Had I never written this story I would never have written a second novel" (*TS* 11).

Distant Music

Toward the end of James Joyce's "The Dead," Gabriel Conroy stands at the foot of the stairs in his aunts' house and gazes up at his wife, Gretta: "There was grace and mystery in her attitude as if she were a symbol of something. He asked himself what is a woman standing on the stairs in the shadow, listening to distant music, a symbol of. If he were a painter he would paint her in that attitude. . . . *Distant Music* he would call the picture if he were a painter."[1] I am reminded of this scene from Joyce whenever I think of Joan Didion's fiction. Like Gabriel, Didion's characters try to reshape reality, to create an image of life as they would like it to be. The motivation for doing this, of course, lies in their dissatisfaction with the way things are. And yet, because of their lack of any vital connection with the past (not to mention any realistic hope for the future), Didion's characters are, in fact, trapped by the way things are.

This is certainly true of her novels, where the old-guard Californians in *Run River* experience the social convulsions that come with economic expansion; where Maria Wyeth in *Play It as It Lays* suffers the trauma of seeing her childhood home turned into a guided missile range; where Charlotte Douglas in *A Book of Common Prayer* abandons the familiar milieu of North America for the terra incognita of a banana republic near the Equator; and where Inez Victor in *Democracy* completes the frontier journey by caring for the refugees of manifest destiny in Kuala Lumpur. And, as we shall see, the tension between illusion and reality also informs Didion's short stories. Even if those stories are as pedestrian as Didion believes them to be, they nevertheless merit our attention, if only because of the light they shed on the thematic continuity of her writing. In her short fiction, as in her novels, we find characters responding with solipsistic fantasy to their loss of an italicized sense of home.

The principal character in Didion's "Coming Home" is Mary Monroe Sweet, a young free-lance television writer who lives in New York with her philandering husband, Charlie Sloane. It is Mary's return from California, where her writing occasionally takes her, that constitutes the dramatic situation of Didion's story. This homecoming, which is the literal reference of Didion's title, leads only to an exchange of recriminations with a callous and unfaithful husband. Moreover, when Mary remembers her last visit to her childhood home in Kentucky, she realizes that that refuge is lost to her as well. After her father's death and her mother's defection to a suburban community in Florida, there is no one left who remembers Mary's childhood. Consequently, she feels "that in certain respects she had ceased to exist" (*TS* 21). Like the cinematic sex goddess Marilyn Monroe, whose memory Mary's name obliquely evokes, Didion's protagonist is effectively an orphan who fails even in marriage to find love and security and a new sense of home.

Like Maria Wyeth and Charlotte Douglas and, to a lesser extent, Lily McClellan and Inez Victor, Mary places her hopes for the future in the concept of motherhood. (At present, she is pregnant with a child whose birth she anticipates with equal measures of joy and apprehension and whose existence Charlie fails even to acknowledge.) Even before she was married, she had pinned a baby-food advertisement beside her bed and had pretended that the baby in the ad was hers. When last we see Mary Monroe Sweet she is lying numbly in bed, on the cold morning of her homecoming, wrapped (as Marilyn Monroe might have been) in a warm fog of phenobarbitol and Pernod—singing to the baby in the baby-food ad the songs her father had once sung to her. In the images of her father (but one in a long line of strong Didion patriarchs) and her imaginary child, Mary is caught between two dreams—one dead, the other powerless to be born.

In "The Welfare Island Ferry," the second of Joan Didion's stories from the sixties, we have a standard situation in her fiction—a bewildered and sensitive woman who has fallen under the spell of an alternately charming and malignant man. The woman—Miss Louisa Patterson Pool—is from Marin County, California, and her lover—Miller Hardin—from Biloxi, Mississippi. They meet at a Friday night party in New York in the early spring and spend the weekend in a series of apartments located in several states. By Monday they arrive at an unspoken agreement to stay together, and by June, Louisa "was convinced that she, who had never before needed anyone, could not have slept without Miller Hardin" (*TS* 33).

On that first Monday Louisa and Miller end up in the West Village apartment of an absent woman. On the bathroom wall of the apartment Louisa sees a framed photograph of Miller, "an enlarged snapshot that showed him sitting in a lawn chair near a river" (*TS* 32). She imagines this picture to have been taken on the eastern shore of Maryland, because that region represents for her a kind of upper-class order and decorum. Like Mary Monroe Sweet, Louisa uses a photograph to connect herself imaginatively to a world that is both desired and functionally inaccessible.

The imagined world of the eastern shore is probably not all that different from Louisa's idealized memory of her own past. When she recalls her childhood, for example, she thinks of "the apparently golden girl she had been." (Although "she later recalled that at sixteen she had considered suicide with a length of garden hose and her mother's station wagon," she "managed to abandon this version of herself in favor of the other" [TS 36].) What she cannot gainsay even in her imagination, however, is that the lost world of her upper-middle-class Northern California girlhood is far removed from that of her present life with Miller.

As it turns out, the West Village apartment to which Miller brings Louisa at the conclusion of their first weekend together belongs to his sister Barbara. He had found Barbara's unconscious body there on Friday morning and had carried her to the hospital. No reason is given for Barbara's suicide, but on Monday Miller insists that Louisa accompany him to a requiem mass at Saint Ignatius Loyola Church. He still remembers some surface amenities, telling Louisa that she must find something with which to cover her head, but he is generally out of place. Neither kneeling nor standing, he slouches awkwardly in his pew and afterward stumbles out of the church in a daze. As a Southerner in New York and a nonpracticing Catholic, Miller Hardin is separated from his past—both cultural and religious.

At one point in the story, Louisa manages briefly to get in touch with an East Coast equivalent of her past. When Miller orders her to spend some time away from the apartment where they now live, she stays for a weekend on Long Island Sound with the family of an old flame named Henry Taylor. The enchantment, however, is short-lived. By Sunday it is raining, a string has snapped on the piano on which Henry's thirteen-year-old twin sisters have shown Louisa how the chords of "Blue Moon," "Once in a While," and "Heart and Soul" coincide, and the twins themselves are arguing over a game of gin rummy. Louisa, knowing that it is time to leave, makes an excuse to return early to New York and to Miller.

When she gets back to her apartment the familiar, tired ritual of argument and complaint resumes. Her final point of contention with Miller involves his spur-of-the-monent plan that they catch the last ferry to Welfare Island and back. When Louisa reminds her lover that he informed her only a few days earlier that the Welfare Island Ferry had ceased to run, he reveals how tenuous is his grip on reality by accusing *Louisa* of a lack of character. Later that night Louisa lies awake in Miller's arms, thinking of Welfare Island and of all the other places they will never go (though presumably not of why she feels compelled to stay with this creep). The story ends just before dawn when Miller whispers to Louisa, *"Hold onto me,"* and she does.

Like "Coming Home" and "The Welfare Island Ferry," "When Did Music Come This Way?" deals with a woman whose past and future seem distinctly unreal and who, in her own words, is trying desperately to "hold on" in the present. Didion's unnamed protagonist tells her story in the first person and addresses the reader directly. "I wish that memory made no connections," she says, "for I would like to tell you about it straight, would like you to see it as finished and self-contained as a painting on a gallery wall; would like *you* to interpret it to *me*" (*TS* 43). What she would like for the reader to interpret to her are the events of a Christmas evening from her childhood in Reno.

As a girl the narrator would celebrate Christmas with her family, a group that included her cousin Cary, her Aunt Inez, and whomever her Aunt Inez happened to be married to at the time. On the Christmas of 1945, Aunt Inez's husband was a flier named Ward, a heavy drinker who would stay away for long periods of time and who did not arrive that Christmas until late on the night of the twenty-fifth. Earlier that evening the narrator and Cary had had an argument, during which Cary accidentally dropped the music box her cousin had given her for Christmas. After her attempts to console Cary prove ineffectual, the narrator goes downstairs to sleep on the sofa behind the Christmas tree. There, the denouement of the story occurs as Didion's narrator—like the protagonists of James Joyce's "Araby" and Sherwood Anderson's "I Want to Know Why"—experiences loss of innocence through a vicarious encounter with adult sexuality.[2]

After she has been on the sofa for a while, the narrator notices Ward and Aunt Inez sitting across the room, visible through the branches of the tree. Ward leans close to his wife and says: " 'Tell me, Inez. Tell me how much. Tell me what you'd do.' 'Anything,' Aunt Inez said again and again. 'You know what I'd do. Anything.' " The inquisition proceeds despite Inez's pleas for Ward to stop: "Tell me what you'd do for it. . . . Say it out loud. Who would you betray." After Inez fails once again to stop Ward, "there was a silence, and then Aunt Inez said, as if by rote, 'I would betray my mother. I would betray my sister. I would betray Cary' " (*TS* 50).

Throughout the remainder of the story we get periodic glimpses of the narrator's present life. We learn, for example, that her marriage is in ruins. (Like Mary Monroe Sweet, she is married to a sadistic jerk named Charlie.) We also learn that in the intervening years Ward has died—killed in a South Dakota aerial show in 1945—and that Aunt Inez has never remarried. The narrator had told us at the outset of the story that—at thirty-three—she has reached the age "as has Cary," where two drinks before lunch can blur her looks. At the end of the story we learn that she has recently had lunch with her cousin. Cary, who has married twice, "had five vodka martinis, one in lieu of dessert" (*TS* 51).

Probably the most puzzling question about this story is the relevance of its title. "When did music come this way? / Children dear, was it yesterday?" is a quotation from Matthew Arnold's "The Forsaken Merman." This poem is a monologue in which the speaker—a mythic creature from the sea—laments the fact that his human wife, Margaret, has deserted him and their children to return to her former home on land. There are certain rough parallels between this narrative and Didion's story. To begin with, Inez, although she may never actually desert her family, does concede to Ward her willingness to do so. (Unlike the merman's wife, who is lured away from her maternal loyalty by church bells, Inez is prey to a more elemental temptation.) Also, one of the most memorable scenes in Arnold's poem follows the merman and his children from the sea to the village church, where they find the praying Margaret with her eyes fixed not on them but "seal'd to the holy book." The denouement of Didion's story occurs when the narrator peeks undetected at Aunt Inez paying obeisance to Ward. The repetitive, ritualistic quality of their conversation (anticipating something that Ivan Costello tries to force Maria Wyeth to say in *Play It as It Lays*) resembles nothing so much as a private liturgy.

Another line of speculation might identify Ward with the merman, himself. There is a kind of mythic aloofness about Ward. He is removed from the rest of the family, the narrator tells us. ("I do not mean that he disliked us; we simply failed to touch him" [*TS* 46].) And when she tries to remember Ward, she "can call up only cartoon characters: Smilin' Jack, Steve Canyon, the nameless flier in love with Lace" (*TS* 45). Finally, Ward is like Arnold's merman in that neither is at home on earth: one swims in the sea, the other soars on the air. Perhaps we ought not to push this comparison too far, however. Margaret forsakes the merman as well as her children, whereas Ward (or his sexuality) is Inez's sole object of fidelity, that for which she would betray all others.

Probably the safest assertion we can make is that the sense of nostalgia, loss, and pathos that pervades Arnold's poem conveys precisely the tone Didion seeks in her story. By alluding to "The Forsaken Merman" in her title she may be attempting to deepen the resonance of that tone. And more concretely, the breaking of the music box serves as a symbolic sundering of the harmonies of childhood and of home. It is a theme repeated in Didion's fiction with the insistence of a broken record. In each of her stories, the happiness and security of an imagined past fade in and out of the mind like distant music. "When did music come this way?" her characters ask. Perhaps it was yesterday, surely not today, probably not tomorrow.

Chapter Nine
Not Exactly Locusts

Given the fact that Joan Didion and John Gregory Dunne have spent most of their adult lives in and around the motion picture industry, it is not surprising that they have occasionally written about the significance of Hollywood in American culture. In order to understand Didion's place in the literature of Hollywood, however, it is necessary to appreciate the fact that ever since the mid-thirties that literature has been dominated by two exaggerated images of the film capital. The first, and more familiar, depicts Hollywood as the realization of the American dream. For millions like Dallas Beardsley, it is an enchanted city where a lucky few can rise not only from rags to riches but from obscurity to fame.

For many others, however, Hollywood is less Eldorado than a fool's paradise, epitome of everything that is venal and meretricious in American life. The image of what Didion and Dunne call "Hollywood the Destroyer" is as much an article of faith for highbrow cynics as the original myth of enchantment is for the *naifs* who inhabit the invisible city. This negative image is largely the creation of disillusioned writers who came west for big bucks with the introduction of sound into motion pictures in the thirties and remained to debunk the scam that fed them. Anyone who has read a "Hollywood novel" knows that just as every thesis produces an antithesis, so too does every myth generate an antimyth.

The great offense that Didion, Dunne, and other recent revisionists have committed against our national pieties is to find a middle ground between those who regard California as "a wet dream in the mind of New York" and those who see it as a place where the only cultural advantage is the ability to turn right on a red light.[1] The new realism purveyed by these revisionists essentially seeks to *demythologize* Hollywood, to see it as neither heaven nor hell but as a company town where real people live and work. This dialectical process has produced what for lack of a better term we might call an anti-antimyth. Such a position was perhaps best expressed by John Gregory Dunne when an editor for the *Atlantic* asked him why he wrote for the movies. "Because," Dunne said, "the money is good. Because doing a screenplay is like doing a combination jigsaw-and-crossword puzzle; it's not writing, but it can be fun. And because the other night, after a screening, we went out to a party with Mike Nichols and Candice Bergen and Warren Beatty and Barbra Steisand. I never did that at *Time*."[2]

Schmucks with Underwoods

In her film criticism and other writings about Hollywood, Joan Didion exhibits an uncompromisingly antielitist sensibility. Although she is not exactly a tinsel enthusiast, she has little regard for the rarefied tastes of such fashionable critics as Stanley Kauffmann, John Simon, and Pauline Kael. In reading through her movie reviews, particularly her regular column for *Vogue* (1 January 1964–15 February 1966), one is struck by Didion's willingness to defend the popular and attack the chic: she praises *Dr. Zhivago* and *The Unsinkable Molly Brown,* while finding serious fault with Carl Foreman's *The Victors* and Sidney Lumet's *The Pawnbroker.* (The same predilection has caused her to perform a more recent hatchet job on the eminent Woody Allen.[3])

The first of Didion's columns for *Vogue* gives us a fairly clear idea of the sorts of films she admires. "I make excuses to be home," she writes, "whenever Wendell Corey is slithering in and out of *The Big Knife* on the Late Show; I pull up the covers and settle in with mindless delight when Katharine Hepburn sweeps into *The Philadelphia Story.* I weep when James Stewart brings *The Spirit of St. Louis* in over the coast of Ireland, weep when Joel McCrea tells America how The Lights Are Going Out All Over Europe Tonight in *Foreign Correspondent;* weep even when James Mason flounders into the surf at Malibu in the Judy Garland *A Star Is Born.*"[4]

In her 1973 essay "In Hollywood" Didion advances the unconventional notion that Hollywood is "the last extant stable society." Her point is that for the sort of insider typified by Cecilia Brady in Fitzgerald's *The Last Tycoon,* the rituals of doing business in the film capital are as complex and inflexible as the rules of a high-stakes card game. "The place makes everyone a gambler," she writes. "It's spirit is speedy, obsessive, immaterial. . . . The action is everything, more consuming than sex, more immediate than politics; more important always than the acquisition of money, which is never, for the gambler, the true point of the exercise" (*WA* 159–60).

The problem with so many people who write about Hollywood is that they "seem so temperamentally at odds with what both Fellini and Truffaut have called the 'circus' aspect of making film that there is flatly no question of their ever apprehending the social and emotional reality of the process" (*WA* 163). The result is that such persons tend to approach film as literature rather than as the combination jigsaw-and-crossword puzzle Dunne describes it as being. Often motion picture production is less the result of collaboration than of protracted conflict. To determine creative responsibility for a film, it is more important to know who had the final cut than who conceived the original story. The identity of the *auteur* is to be found not in the film's credits but in its deal memo.

Because Hollywood is a one-industry town, those who have survived its perils have maintained a greater sense of cultural cohesiveness than is to be had in most other communities. Didion cites the dinner given in honor of Adolph "Papa" Zukor's one-hundredth birthday as a case in point. "Many of those present have had occasion over the years to regard Adolph 'Papa' Zukor with some rancor," she writes, "but on this night there is among them a resigned warmth, a recognition that they will attend one another's funerals" (*WA* 161).

The essay in which Didion most directly attacks the Hollywood antimyth (although she does not call it that) is "I Can't Get That Monster Out of My Mind" (1964). Here she is not trying to convey an insider's view of the film capital so much as to dispel what she considers to be the false view of "Hollywood the Destroyer." According to that false view, the American motion picture industry "represents a kind of mechanical monster, programmed to stifle and destroy all that is interesting and worthwhile and 'creative' in the human spirit." Didion seems to regard those who promote such a view in much the same light as Jack Warner viewed writers in general—as Schmucks with Under-woods. It is these schmucks who have conditioned us "to recall the brightest minds of a generation, deteriorating around the swimming pool at the Garden of Allah while they waited for calls from the Thalberg Building" (*STB* 150).

Not only is the image of "Hollywood the Destroyer" a distortion of reality, but the reality being distorted isn't even current. The old studio system may or may not have been oppressive, but it is now clearly a thing of the past. Although we have finally reached the millennium yearned for by critics of the Hollywood monster, the time when fewer but better movies can be made, Didion contends that only half of that vision has been realized. We now have fewer but not necessarily better movies. One reason for this is that "American directors, with a handful of exceptions, are not much interested in style, . . . [but] are at heart didactic" (*STB* 153). Thus, when they are given creative freedom, the result is all too often an exercise in moral pomposity. As an example, Didion cites Stanley Kramer's *Judgment at Nuremberg*. This film, made in 1961, "was an intrepid indictment not of authoritarianism in the abstract, not of the trials themselves, not of the various moral and legal issues involved, but of Nazi war atrocities, about which there would have seemed already to be some consensus" (*STB* 154).

Didion concludes her essay by suggesting that the current malaise in Hollywood may be due less to the monster itself than to the creative banality of those who seek to realize their private fantasies on the motion picture screen. She tells us, for example, of running into a producer "who complained to me of the difficulties he had working within what I recognized as the System, although he did not call it that. He longed, he said, to do an adaptation of a certain Charles Jackson short story. 'Some really terrific stuff' he said. 'Can't touch it, I'm afraid. About masturbation' " (*STB* 156).

Plenty of *Nothing*

Despite the image of the movie capital we find in Didion's Hollywood essays, the ambience of her Hollywood novel, *Play It as It Lays,* is anything but that of the "last extant stable society." Instead, we seem to have in this novel the tawdry and nihilistic setting of traditional antimyth fiction, a setting where the cultural disintegration that began to occur in *Run River* is already an accomplished fact. Here, a young third-rate actress named Maria Wyeth daily climbs into a Corvette and drives the Los Angeles freeways, where the act of making complicated lane changes is the only ritual that can bring order to an otherwise chaotic life.[5]

When Maria is introduced, she is remembering the events of the novel from the perspective of a mental institution. A native of Silver Wells, Nevada (a former mining community that is now the site of a nuclear test range), Maria is separated from her obnoxiously cruel husband, Carter Lang, and from her brain-damaged daughter, Kate. (Al-

though Maria feels genuine maternal love for Kate, the child's condition makes it nearly impossible for that love to be demonstrated or
returned.) When Maria once again becomes pregnant (probably by a
man named Les Goodwin), Carter pressures her into having an abortion
by threatening that he will otherwise prevent her from seeing the
institutionalized Kate. Following her abortion and other, lesser, trau-
mas, Maria finds herself in bed with Carter's producer BZ. The purpose, however, is not love but death. BZ (who is a homosexual and thus
not erotically interested in Maria) swallows a handful of Seconal and
dies in Maria's comforting arms. Rather than follow his example, she
keeps on living.

The physical appearance of *Play It as It Lays* is structured so that the
reader's response is in large part subliminal and nonrational. In her
essay "Why I Write" Didion says that her technical intention in this
novel was to write "a book in which anything that happened would
happen off the page, a 'white' book to which the reader would have to
bring his or her own bad dreams."[6] Told in eighty-seven chapters,
covering 214 pages (some of which are as short as a single paragraph),
Play It as It Lays does its best to instill a sense of vertigo in the reader.
As Guy Davenport points out, Didion "has given the novel a pace so
violent and so powerful that its speed becomes the dominant symbol of
her story."[7]

The narrative focus of Didion's second novel is more limited, and
hence more controlled, than that of *Run River*. (Alfred Kazin goes so far
as to suggest that when her control becomes too obvious, Didion turns
herself into a kind of literary *director auteur*.[8] Although the bulk of the
story is narrated from a third-person limited perspective, the novel
begins with first-person accounts by Maria; BZ's wife, Helene; and
Carter, and ends with seven of the final sixteen chapters being narrated
by Maria. Structurally, these first-person narrations are probably not
well enough integrated into the rest of the novel. (Kazin is right to
point out that "Maria would hardly ask . . . 'Why should a coral snake
need two glands of neurotoxic poison to survive when a king snake, *so
similarly marked,* needs none. Where is the Darwinian logic there?' "[9]
Still, these first-person monologues constitute a relatively small propor-
tion of the entire novel. The third-person point of view, which is much
more dominant, is also far more effective. Through it Didion is able to
move quite easily between a close identification with Maria and an
ironic distance from her.

Another technical device used to good effect is the development of theme through a cinematic equivalent of the theater trope that presents life as a staged drama.[10] Consider, for example, the two movies in which Maria appears. The first of these—a cinema verité picture called *Maria*—follows its subject through a typical day in New York: "At the end she was thrown into negative and looked dead" (*PL* 20). This film runs for seventy-four minutes, has won a prize at a festival in Eastern Europe, and has never been released. Maria's second picture—*Angel Beach*—is a bike movie in which she is raped by the members of a motorcycle gang. Maria enjoys watching this second film because "the girl on the screen seemed to have a definite knack for controlling her own destiny" (*PL* 20), whereas she feels that the girl in the first picture "had no knack for anything" (*PL* 21).

Like so many within the moral environment of Hollywood, Maria comes to define herself in terms of artifice. For her, as for the protagonist of Walker Percy's *The Moviegoer,* films "certify" reality. At one point in the novel she is able to sleep only after seeing herself in a television drama. And when she thinks of the happy family that she and her husband and their daughter will never be, she thinks of an imaginary home movie: "Carter throwing a clear plastic ball filled with confetti, Kate missing the ball. Kate crying. Carter swinging Kate by her wrists. The spray from the sprinklers and the clear plastic ball with the confetti falling inside and Kate's fat arms stretched up again for the catch she would always miss. Freeze frame. . . . On film they might have seemed a family" (*PL* 137–38).

If Maria's present home life is an off-screen disaster, she also lacks any real-life connections with her childhood home. When she was nine, her father lost his house in a card game and moved the family from Reno to the smaller Nevada town of Silver Wells ("pop. then 28, now 0"). A prospective boom town that never materialized, Silver Wells is now a barren desert, a test range for doomsday weapons. With both her parents dead (her mother's body was torn apart by coyotes after an automobile accident), Maria's ties with her past have been so irrevocably severed that she is unable to "go back" even under hypnosis.

In addition to domestic unhappiness, Maria is bedeviled by a type of sexual conflict that is not only common in Didion's fiction, but also pervades much of American literature. In *Love and Death in the American Novel,* Leslie Fiedler speaks of the apparent schizophrenia that informs perceptions of sexual identity in this country. Fiedler argues that just as women are frequently viewed as either virgin or whore, earth-mother or bitch-goddess, so too are men often depicted in terms of two extremes—as gentleman or seducer, rational suitor or demon lover. In *Run River,* Didion had Lily Knight McClellan torn equally between the Apollonian Everett and the Dionysian Ryder. In *Play It as It Lays,* she stacks her deck by giving Maria Wyeth's single Apollonian lover three Dionysian rivals.

What is perhaps the most grotesque scene in the novel occurs when Maria encounters one of these Dionysian types, an egocentric young actor named Johnny Waters, at a decadent Hollywood party. Waters is the sort of individual who plays "Midnight Hour" repeatedly on the tape deck of his car, mistakenly calls Maria "Myra," and suggests that she "do it with a Coke bottle" when she initially rejects his sexual advances. Later, when he does get his way with her, he breaks an amyl nitrite popper under his nose just prior to orgasm, tells Maria not to move, and orders her to wake him in three hours—"with your tongue" (*PL* 153). And so disappears the old D. H. Lawrence salvation-through-sex motif.

Another one of Maria's Dionysian lovers is the vaguely demonic Ivan Costello. Because he lives in New York, Ivan is mostly a memory or a voice on the telephone. Prior to her abortion, Maria dreams that she has given birth to her baby and that she and the baby and Kate are all living with Ivan Costello. Later, however, we learn that when she *had* been with Ivan, he had made it quite clear that he would never marry her and that he would insist on her aborting any child she might conceive. He now calls her in the middle of the night and, like Ward in "When Did Music Come This Way?," asks, "How much do you want it. . . . Tell me what you'd do to get it from me" (*PL* 71).

If anything, Maria's relationship with her husband is even more destructive than her encounters with Johnny Waters and Ivan Costello. Like Johnny and Ivan, Carter Lang is a self-centered hedonist who treats Maria solely as an object. He is the director who has made both of her movies, and when he thinks of her, it is invariably in cinematic terms. When Didion allows him to speak in his own voice at the beginning of the novel, he remembers his life with Maria as a series of unpleasant scenes. "I played and replayed these scenes and others like them," he recalls, "composing them as if for the camera, trying to find some order, a pattern. I found none" (*PL* 14).

As his name would imply, Maria's Apollonian lover Les Goodwin is a better but weaker man than the other males in her life. After her abortion, Maria fantasizes an idyllic future in which she and Les and Kate live in a house by the sea. Here, everything is clean and orderly and in touch with nature. Kate (miraculously normal) does lessons at a big pine table, and all three members of the imaginary family drink cold white wine and eat the mussels they have gathered on the beach. "But by dawn [Maria] was always back in the house in Beverly Hills, uneasy in the queer early light, . . . [where she understood] that the still center of the daylight world was never a house by the sea but the corner of Sunset and La Brea. In that empty sunlight Kate could do no lessons, and the mussels on any shore that Maria knew were toxic" (*PL* 115).

Upon first reading *Play It as It Lays,* one is likely to be struck by its spare, bleak, nihilistic tone. What becomes evident with successive readings, however, is the crucial function that irony and humor serve in this novel. One of the most hideously black comic scenes in *Play It as It Lays,* the contact between Maria and the man who is to take her to the abortionist, is also one of the most memorable in contemporary fiction. Maria meets her contact, a moral zombie in white duck pants, under the big red "T" at the local Thriftimart. To pass the time he hums "I Get a Kick Out of You" and begins to make inane small talk. Speaking of the neighborhood through which they are passing, he says, "Nice homes here. Nice for kids." He then asks Maria whether she gets good mileage on her car and proceeds to compare the merits of his Cadillac with those of a Camaro he is contemplating buying: "Maybe that sounds like a step down, a Cad to a Camaro," he says, "but I've got my eye on this *particular* Camaro, exact model of the pace car in the Indianapolis 500" (*PL* 79).

Because Maria has strong maternal instincts, her abortion is the cause of much guilt and anxiety. It can also be seen as a symbol of the breakdown of the family and of traditional standards of morality. Yet what makes the episode of the abortion unforgettable is the image of that cretin in white duck pants babbling about the mileage Maria gets on her car. Throughout *Play It as It Lays,* Didion employs just such comic touches to undercut the sentimental, self-pitying nihilism inherent in Maria's story.

Nowhere is this ironic distance between Didion as author and Maria as character more crucial than in the novel's climactic scene. As BZ is dying in Maria's arms, the juke box in a bar across the way is playing "King of the Road," Roger Miller's country music formulation of the play-it-as-it-lays philosophy. BZ has asked and answered what Albert Camus regarded as the one serious philosophical question—"judging whether life is or is not worth living."[11] Having resolved that question in the negative, BZ says to Maria, "You're still playing. . . . Some day you'll wake up and you just won't feel like playing any more" (*PL* 212). Apparently BZ sees suicide as a last significant act of defiance. If life cannot be improved, he seems to say, then at least it can be ended. But for Maria such an attitude amounts to a pathetic kind of pose. She even ridicules BZ's taking an overdose of pills as "a queen's way of doing it" (*PL* 212).

Unlike BZ, Maria is averse to examining life—philosophically or otherwise. (At the outset of the novel she says, "What makes Iago evil? some people ask. I never ask" [*PL* 3].) She tells us that she keeps on living because she hopes to get Kate back someday and go some place where they can live simply. Maria will do some canning and be a mother to her child. (Significantly, her pastoral dream no longer includes Les Goodwin, whose wimpish inability to prevent Maria's abortion disqualifies him as a prospective husband and father.) This "hope" is cause for optimism, however, only if there is a chance of its being realized. Yet, by the end of the novel, we understand that Maria's dream is simply a last-ditch act of self-delusion. Viewed in this light, the closing lines of *Play It as It Lays* seem ironic indeed. Maria tells us: "*I know something Carter never knew, or Helene, or maybe you. I know what 'nothing' means, and keep on playing. Why, BZ would say. Why not, I say,*" (*PL* 214). Maria may actually believe she is living for Kate; however, the truth, as Didion's narrative perspective forces us to see it, is that Maria continues to live because, deep down, she does not even share BZ's faith in the meaningfulness of death.

John Barth's Todd Andrews comes to much the same conclusion at the end of *The Floating Opera*. Todd writes in his journal: "*There's no final reason for living [or for suicide].*" And a bit later, he says: "To realize that nothing makes any final difference is overwhelming; but if one goes no farther and becomes a saint, a cynic, or a suicide on principle, one hasn't reasoned completely. The truth is that nothing makes any difference, including that truth. Hamlet's question is, absolutely, meaningless."[12] For Todd Andrews and Maria Wyeth, there are *no* significant philosophical problems.

If there is one metaphysical perception that does inform Maria's approach to life, it is suggested by the title of the novel. "*Always when I play back my father's voice,*" Maria recalls, "*it is with a professional rasp, it goes as it lays, don't do it the hard way. My father advised me that life itself was a crap game: it was one of two lessons I learned as a child. The other was that overturning a rock was apt to reveal a rattlesnake. As lessons go those two seem to hold up, but not to apply"* (PL 200).

In expecting to find a snake under every rock, Maria is symbolically acknowledging the pervasiveness of evil in an essentially hostile universe.[13] (She has suggested earlier that it is a universe in which one cannot even count on Darwinian logic to prevail.) So, how does one live in such an environment? By playing it as it lays, by never taking the hard way in anything. Although Maria has learned this lesson in childhood and continues to live by it, she concedes that such stoic acceptance (if that is what it is) doesn't really work. It is simply one arbitrary method among many for dealing with the void in which we are doomed to live. It is a lesson that seems to hold up *"but not to apply."*

In examining Didion's writings about the movie capital, we must finally wonder how to reconcile the relatively benign view of that place we find in her essays with the nightmare vision of her Hollywood novel. To resolve this dilemma we need to understand the difference between Didion's approaches to journalism and to fiction. In her journalism she is trying to tell us what she thinks she knows about a particular subject. But in her fiction she is trying to tell us the stories that certain mental images suggest to her. Let us, then, consider the image that served as the basis for *Play It as It Lays*.

In "Why I Write" Didion recalls having seen a young actress with long hair and a short white halter dress walk "through the casino at the Riviera in Las Vegas at one in the morning. She crosses the casino alone and picks up a house telephone." The author watches this woman "because I have heard her paged, and recognize her name. . . . [But] I know nothing about her. Who is paging her? Why is she here to be paged? How exactly did she come to this?" For Didion, "it was precisely this moment in Las Vegas that made *Play It as It Lays* tell itself to me."[14]

It is important for us as readers to keep this image in mind: not only to see the young woman as Didion sees her, but also to see Didion looking *at* her. In short, to lose sight of the ironic perspective in this novel is inevitably to misread its author's intentions. At one level, Maria's story is one of genuine suffering and despair. Yet, at another level, Didion seems to be writing a parody of the novel of despair. She does this not by minimizing or ridiculing Maria's plight, but by undercutting the kinds of philosophical responses to that plight that romantic-existentialist writers might invoke.

Perhaps we can better understand Didion's attitude here if we consider the treatment of "nothingness"—or *nada*—in one of the most famous works of romantic-existentialist fiction, Ernest Hemingway's "A Clean Well-Lighted Place." According to Carlos Baker, Hemingway's greatest achievement in this story lies in his "development, through the most carefully controlled understatement, of the young waiter's mere *nothing* into the old waiter's Something—a Something called Nothing which is so huge, terrible, overbearing, inevitable, and omnipresent that, once experienced, it can never be forgotten."[15] BZ and Maria have both experienced something very similar to the *nada* of Hemingway's story. BZ responds to that experience by allowing it to become for him a Something called Nothing. Maria, however, is living testament to the fact that Nothing is—in reality—*no thing.*

No, Maria is not Prince Hamlet, nor was she meant to be. Neither is *Play It as It Lays* primarily *about* the Unreal City that is Hollywood. What we have in this novel is a kind of postexistentialist nihilism that not only differs philosophically from the vision of a Hemingway or a Camus, but also obviates the necessity of passing judgment on a region or an industry or—indeed—on anything at all. In her relentless, black-comic detachment from the despair that her novel probes, Joan Didion has reduced the Hollywood antimyth to the level of conscious self-parody. Nathanael West wrote about characters who packed up their shattered dreams and came west to die. Maria Wyeth, having pushed beyond the disillusionment that comes with shattered dreams, has stayed west to live. And that, in the still center of her daylight world, may well be a fate worse than death.

Chapter Ten

The Witness I Wanted to Be

The enthusiastic response to Joan Didion's third novel, *A Book of Common Prayer* (1977), was a mixture of admiration and surprise—as if a highly respected utility infielder had not only won a starting position but also proved himself to be one of the finest shortstops in the league. Everyone knew that Didion was a superb journalist, but it was easy to dismiss her fiction as the minor work of a brilliant stylist. For example, those few who actually bothered to read *Run River* could write it off as highbrow soap opera of the sort that lends spurious distinction to the glossier women's magazines (the accumulation of status details alone—right down to the character of China Mary, the McClellans' oriental mammy—defines a world in which uppity wetbacks and Okies, as well as aerospace engineers, are seen as a social menace). Although *Play It as It Lays* demonstrated a greater technical sophistication, it struck many as too much of a tour de force. After all, when you know what *nothing* means, what do you do for an encore?

Even if the seeds of *A Book of Common Prayer* had been sown in Didion's earlier work, few in the literary world expected so bountiful a harvest. Here was the feel for contemporary American life so evident in Didion's essays and so lacking in her first two novels. Here also was a more complex manipulation of style than we had seen before. (Perhaps *Play It as It Lays* had simply been a pyrotechnical warmup for the main event.) Moreover, the elegiac mood of *Run River* had been purged of sentimentality by what Didion had learned to do in "When Did Music Come This Way?": "to make narrative tension out of nothing more than the juxtaposition of past and present." To be sure, there were a few who thought *A Book of Common Prayer* mannered and idiosyncratic, though in a less obvious way than *Play It as It Lays,* but those nay-sayers were drowned out by the general chorus of approval for Didion's third novel. As we shall see, the many who praised this book and the few who panned it together tell us something pertinent about the virtues of Joan Didion's craft and the limitations of her sensibility.

Una Turista

The present-tense action of *A Book of Common Prayer* is set in the imaginary Central American republic of Boca Grande ("Big Mouth"), which is to say that it transpires in a sinister social void. (In the "Letters from Central America" that Didion's protagonist Charlotte tries unsuccessfully to sell to the *New Yorker* she refers to Boca Grande as a "land of contrasts"; however, Didion's narrator, Grace, informs us that this country is, in fact, "relentlessly the same."[1]) Grace Strasser-Mendana, née Tabor, is our guide to Boca Grande as well as our witness to the life and death of Charlotte Douglas. Grace is a sixty-year-old anthropologist who has married into one of the nation's three or four solvent families. Her husband's death has left her "in putative control of fifty-nine-point-eight percent of the arable land and about the same percentage of the decision-making process in Boca Grande" (*BCP* 18–19). It is in Boca Grande that Grace meets Charlotte Douglas and begins to learn of her confused and pointless life.

Charlotte's story is a deceptively simple one: "she left one man, she left a second man, she traveled again with the first; she let him die alone. She lost one child to 'history' and another to 'complications' . . . ; she imagined herself capable of shedding that baggage and came to Boca Grande, a tourist" (*BCP* 11). Like so many of Didion's characters Charlotte is a westerner—from Hollister, California. She spends two years at Berkeley, where she meets and marries an untenured English instructor named Warren Bogart. Perversely charming and a bit sadistic, Warren is the first of the men whom Charlotte leaves. He is also the father of the child she loses to history.

Although she is only a minor character in her own right, that child—Marin Bogart—plays a significant role in her mother's story by deeply affecting Charlotte's psyche. Marin derives much of her credibility from the reader's assumed knowledge of radical youth politics of the late 1960s and early 1970s, particularly of the Patricia Hearst case. Marin comes from a relatively conventional upper-middle-class background and appears to be a dull, unremarkable adolescent. At sixteen, she "had been photographed with her two best friends wearing the pink-and-white candy-striped pinafores of Children's Hospital volunteers, and had later abandoned her Saturdays at the hospital as 'too sad.' " But at eighteen this same child of the middle class "had been observed with her four best friends detonating a crude pipe bomb in the lobby of the Transamerica Building at 6:30 A.M., hijacking a

P.S.A. L-1011 at San Francisco Airport and landing it at Wendover, Utah, where they burned it in time for the story to interrupt the network news and disappeared" (*BCP* 58).

After Marin's disappearance Charlotte conceives another child, this time by her second husband—Leonard Douglas—a prominent San Francisco attorney who specializes in defending radical causes. She then leaves Leonard to return to Warren Bogart, and together she and Warren travel through the modern South, where they stay at a succession of cheap motels after wearing out their welcome with a host of Warren's friends and casual acquaintances. Charlotte finally leaves Warren a second time and returns to New Orleans, where she gives birth prematurely to a hydrocephalic child "devoid of viable liver function" (*BCP* 147). The child dies in Yucatán and Charlotte flees without rational aim to Boca Grande, hoping someday to be reunited with Marin, for "in a certain dim way Charlotte believed that she had located herself at the very cervix of the world, the place through which a child lost to history must eventually pass" (*BCP* 197).

While in Boca Grande Charlotte tries to live her life oblivious to the random political violence that surrounds her. But finally Charlotte Douglas is herself lost to history. She is shot in one of the periodic shifts in power that constitute the only "history" that Boca Grande has ever known. Grace sees that Charlotte's body is placed in a coffin and is flown back to San Francisco. Since she is unable to find a flag with which to drape the coffin, Grace purchases a child's T-shirt, which is printed like an American flag, but which lacks the correct number of stars and stripes. The novel closes with Grace pondering the enigma that was Charlotte Douglas while awaiting her own imminent death by pancreatic cancer.

Although Charlotte Douglas's story is one of classic American innocence, she is not the sort of *naif* Henry James used to send to Europe, nor does she exactly resemble the self-conscious expatriates of Hemingway. Her most frequently cited literary progenitor is not a foreign traveler at all but Gatsby gone east.[2] However, even here there are crucial differences as well as similarities. To begin with, for Charlotte there is no literal East as there is for Gatsby. (It is true that Marin does hide out in Buffalo when she is on the lam from the law, but that is not so much a mythic East as a mythic nowhere and, in any event, a hideout that Charlotte never finds.) If Gatsby's journey from his native Midwest to Long Island is primarily one of space, Charlotte's odyssey from her girlhood on a California ranch to her jetset life as Mrs. Leonard

Douglas is one of time. The San Francisco in which she lives as an adult may be geographically west, but culturally it is indistinguishable from Manhattan and other points east. Far from being a dreamland for Charlotte, it is, in Warren Bogart's pithy characterization, a land of Arabs and Jews.

By most objective standards Charlotte's life with Leonard Douglas would seem to be reasonably happy. Leonard is successful, even-tempered, and genuinely interested in his wife's welfare. Warren Bogart, on the other hand, is none of these things. But Leonard finally seems too decent, too rational, and too liberal ever to satisfy the self-martyred romantic in Charlotte. Although Didion tries hard not to caricature Leonard, he seems all too typical of a certain "radical chic" sensibility. He has been in analysis for eight years, and his psychiatrist, Polly Orben, "frequently reported that they were within a year or so of 'terminating' or 'ending' " (BCP 71). He even keeps marijuana in a silver music box that plays "Puff the Magic Dragon." According to Warren, Leonard and Charlotte do not have a life together; they have a "life-style."

For reasons known only to herself, Charlotte abandons this life-style to return to Warren. He apparently possesses for her a demonic appeal not unlike that displayed by the other Dionysian males in Didion's fiction. His personality is so vivid, in fact, that Warren tends to dominate every scene he is in. We may not understand Charlotte's attraction to Warren, but he is a thoroughly believable scoundrel: "Like many Southerners and like some Catholics and unlike Charlotte he was raised to believe not in 'hard work' or 'self-reliance' but in the infinite power of the personal appeal, the request for a favor, the intervention of one or another merciful Virgin. He had an inchoate but definite conviction that access to the mysteries of good fortune was arranged in the same way as access to the Boston Club, a New Orleans institution to which he did not belong but always had a guest card" (BCP 162–63).

When Charlotte leaves Leonard Douglas and she and Warren head South, it is ostensibly to visit a dying relative who has played sugar daddy to many of Warren's ill-fated business and cultural ventures. As it turns out, it is not that relative but Warren himself who is dying. He spends his last months drinking himself senseless, abusing Charlotte and other (multiple) sexual partners, and generally annoying everyone with whom he comes in contact. What makes Warren perversely appealing, however, is his sheer verbal brilliance. To find an equally literate quality of malice in modern American writing, one must turn to Edward Albee's *Who's Afraid of Virginia Woolf?*. But unlike Albee's characters, Warren has no rival among his peers for either wit or venom. His victims are frequently passive and almost always inarticulate.

Beyond Charlotte's native West and the easternized West of her adult life, there are two other regional settings in Didion's novel. One is the modern South through which Warren and Charlotte travel. This is not the traditional South of William Faulkner or Eudora Welty, but the Sunbelt South satirically depicted in the fiction of Walker Percy. The gentility and graciousness that once characterized the region have degenerated into such transparently forced civility that one of her hosts can say to Charlotte, "The idea, your friend Warren going off and leaving you here alone, might not matter to you but it matters to me, a man insults a lady in my house and he insults me. You wouldn't understand that, Mrs. Douglas, I'm certain it's all free and easy where your people come from" (*BCP* 180).

One suspects that the reason Warren enjoys traveling in the South is that Southerners are more easily offended than are the cosmopolitan inhabitants of Leonard Douglas's world. ("His favorite hand was outrageousness," Grace tells us; "in a fluid world like Leonard Douglas's where no one could be outraged Warren Bogart was dimmed, confused, unable to operate" [*BCP* 162].) When Charlotte complains to Warren about the treatment they have received, he accuses her of being insufficiently familiar with "normal people," of being too used to Arabs and Jews. To this Charlotte replies, "I can't help noticing Arabs and Jews are rather less insulting to their houseguests." "Not to this houseguest they wouldn't be, babe," Warren responds. "You show me an Arab who'll put up with me, I'll show you an Arab who doesn't get the picture" (*BCP* 180–81).

In distinguishing between "normal people," on the one hand, and "Arabs and Jews," on the other, Warren is dealing less in facts than in social attitudes.[3] (Charlotte's brother Dickie refers to Leonard Douglas as "the Jew," although he is not Jewish.) "Normal people" are, by definition, those who respond to Warren in a particular way. (We are told that such people can be found not only in the South, but also in academia and on the Upper East Side of New York.) For "normal people," Warren is a charming boor, a witty iconoclast whom they love to hate. (They see him as an updated version of Alexander Woolcott with a bit of the Marquis de Sade thrown in for good measure.) However, for "Arabs and Jews" he is simply a tired, irrelevant anachronism. They "put up" with him by ignoring him. And to someone of Warren Bogart's sensibility, such tolerance is the unkindest slight of all.

As I have already suggested, the final setting of the novel—Boca Grande—more nearly resembles an antisetting. It is not so much a fully realized Central America as it is a touchstone against which Didion can define life among the *norteamericanas*. It makes a certain iconographical sense that Charlotte, whom the local studs call the *norteamericana* cunt, should spend her final days in Boca Grande, "the cervix of the world." After all, Charlotte is a woman who avoids the backward glance and Boca Grande is a country without history. ("Every time the sun falls on a day in Boca Grande that day appears to vanish from local memory, to be reinvented if necessary but never recalled" [*BCP* 14].) However, by the end of the novel we realize that Charlotte's North American naivete is nothing short of disastrous in the perverse and cynical environment of Boca Grande. As an ingenuous child of the western United States, she is out of place in a land that lacks a future as well as a past, a land where all time is frozen in a present "relentlessly the same."

Although the novel is full of examples of Charlotte's innocence, my personal favorite involves her compassion for some street children in Boca Grande. She notices that every morning three small children, who apparently do not know how to swim, climb under the fence around the swimming pool at the Caribe Hotel, leap into the deep end of the pool, and flounder and gasp from one side to the next. To complicate matters, there is no lifeguard and the water is green with algae. Although Charlotte could not see the children beneath the surface of the water, she would take her breakfast to the pool every morning to be on hand to keep the children from drowning. (The manager of the Caribe refuses to take any action because there are no children registered at the hotel.) Then one morning, when she can see only two of the three children for thirty straight seconds, Charlotte jumps into the pool—fully clothed and screaming. "She choked and the murky water blinded her and when she came up all three children were standing on the edge of the pool fighting over her [six-hundred-dollar] handbag" (*BCP* 229). These urchins are more worldy-wise than Charlotte will ever be.

If it is not altogether clear why Charlotte has come to Boca Grande, it is even less clear why she stays. At one level her insistence on remaining may simply be another indication of her solipsistic innocence. Despite sufficient warning, she chooses to ignore the danger that surrounds her. When a bomb goes off in the clinic where she works,

Charlotte remembers only that she bled (not from any wounds, but because she was changing a Tampax at the time). In a larger sense, though, her decision to stay in Boca Grande is a gratuitous act of courage. She says to Leonard, *"I walked away from places all my life and I'm not going to walk away from here"* (*BCP* 256). Charlotte's death accomplishes nothing tangible, but in an absurd world one may be able to manage no more than an existential gesture. (The doomed characters in *Play It as It Lays* cannot even do that.) And so Didion seems to be allowing Charlotte to make something of a marginal affirmation. By restoring some nobility to death, she suggests that life itself may not be utterly devoid of meaning.

But that which gives Charlotte's life meaning is finally a delusion so total that it cannot be adequately fathomed by Didion's narrator and can be no more than hinted at by Didion herself. Charlotte is in Boca Grande, ready to sacrifice all, because she is waiting for someone she thinks may need her, just as Gatsby lies on the rubber mattress in his swimming pool waiting for Daisy. Her Daisy, however, is no lover— for Warren is dead and Charlotte refuses Leonard's pleas that she leave with him. Charlotte's platonic conception of herself springs from a loyalty even more elemental than romantic love. Next to "Occupation" on her passport, she has written "Madre." When Charlotte died, Grace tells us, "she cried not for God but for Marin" (*BCP* 268).

Like Gatsby, Charlotte has allowed her romantic imagination to elevate a banal loved one into an object of worship. That this loved one is a daughter should come as no surprise to readers of Didion's earlier fiction, for here we have repeated at another level the maternal tragedy of *Play It as It Lays*. Like Maria Wyeth, Charlotte builds her hopes for the future on a child who is incapable of being reached. Because Marin Bogart does not suffer from as literal a personality disorder as Kate Lang, she would appear to be potentially more accessible to Charlotte than Kate is to Maria. Ultimately, though, Marin lacks the intelligence and the character necessary to deal with the world around her, much less to forge a lasting bond with her mother. Perhaps Warren sums up the girl's character most succinctly when he says, "Marin can't read. She plays a good game of tennis, she's got a nice backhand, good strong hair and an IQ of about 103" (*BCP* 99).

The theme of maternity also comes up in contexts that are not directly related to Charlotte and Marin. In each case we see a distortion or an attenuation of the traditional family structure. Early in the novel, for example, Grace indicates that her son Gerardo is as lost to her as Marin is to Charlotte. Gerardo even refers to his mother by her first name, as if to suggest that the conventional mother-child relationship no longer exists. Another commentary on family structure occurs at a party Charlotte attends shortly after Marin's disappearance. Here an actress who had recently visited Hanoi speaks of "the superior health and beauty of the children there." " 'It's because they aren't raised by their mothers,' the actress said. 'They don't have any of that bourgeois crap laid on them. . . . No mama-papa-baby-nuclear-family bullshit. . . . It's beautiful' " (*BCP* 130). In the colloquial, non-Aristotelian sense of the term, Joan Didion's novels are all domestic tragedies. The family may well be the last institution standing between the individual and the abyss, the last of what sociologists call "mediating structures." If so, the breakdown of the family becomes a kind of synecdoche for the fragmentation of our entire culture.

Rainbow Slick

For readers familiar with Didion's earlier work, *A Book of Common Prayer* must seem like yet another variation on the themes and characters already encountered in *Run River* and *Play It as It Lays*. To be sure, the Marin subplot adds a touch of contemporary "relevance" to the storyline, and the characterization of Warren Bogart is particularly well done. But it is not at the level of ideas or personalities that *A Book of Common Prayer* distinguishes itself. Like so many modernist novels, this one has been more praised for its form than its content. Specifically, in her use of Grace as narrator, Didion has given her book a coherence lacking in the shifting perspectives of her first two novels and an irony that redeems her story from both sentimentality and melodrama. It is a breathtaking technical achievement that may finally be too clever for its own good.

Grace is what Robert Scholes and Robert Kellogg call the "typical Conradian" narrator, a compromise between third-person-omniscient and first-person-protagonist narration. Such a narrator (e.g. Conrad's Marlow, Fitzgerald's Nick Carraway, and even Melville's Ishmael) is an eyewitness who tells another person's story and who seeks to understand that person "through an imaginative sharing of his experience." Contending that "this has been a very fruitful device in modern fiction," Scholes and Kellogg note that "the story of the protagonist becomes the outward sign or symbol of the inward story of the narrator, who learns from his imaginative participation in the other's experience." What this leads to is the sort of meta-fiction in which "the factual or empirical aspect of the protagonist's life becomes subordinated to the narrator's understanding of it." Thus, "not what really happened but the meaning of what the narrator believes to have happened becomes the central preoccupation."[4] By dividing his narrator from his protagonist, the author obviates the "problem of presenting a character with enough crudeness for *hybris* and *hamartia* but enough sensitivity for ultimate discovery and self-understanding."[5]

In Charlotte Douglas, Didion gives us an unreflective protagonist, and in Grace Strasser-Mendana, the woman who chooses to be Charlotte's "witness," an intelligent and sensitive narrator. However, Grace's understanding of the world in which she lives is also severely limited. She approaches the conundrum that is Charlotte Douglas with an impressive background in the social and biological sciences and a long familiarity with the practical realms of business and power politics. And yet her academic training fails to provide her with an adequate understanding of Charlotte, and her worldly wisdom is insufficient to do Charlotte any practical good. Only too late does Grace realize that Leonard Douglas, in his role as jetset revolutionary, has been running the guns that will eventually kill his wife and that her own late husband, Edgar, in his role as local power broker, had caused much of the bloodshed in Boca Grande. All that saves Grace from the charge of terminal obtuseness is the fact that she finally recognizes and frankly confesses her limitations.

At the outset of the novel, after she has introduced herself to us, she says, "I tell you these things about myself only to legitimize my voice. We are uneasy about a story until we know who is telling it. In no other sense does it matter who 'I' am: 'the narrator' plays no motive role in this narrative, nor would I want to. . . . I am interested in Charlotte Douglas only insofar as she passed through Boca Grande, only insofar as the meaning of that sojourn continues to elude me" (*BCP* 21). And at the end of the novel Grace's self-doubt is even more emphatic: "I am less and less certain that this story has been one of delusion," she says. "Unless the delusion was mine. . . . I have not been the witness I wanted to be." (*BCP* 272). Like the Cretan poet Epimenides, who declared that all Cretans were liars, Grace confronts us with a logical paradox. She is a narrator who frankly confesses her own unreliability.

When asked about her technical intention in *A Book of Common Prayer,* Didion pointed to something she had written on a map of Central America: "Surface like rainbow slick, shifting, fall, thrown away, iridescent." "I wanted to do a deceptive surface," she said, "that appeared to be one thing and turned color as you looked through it."[6] The deceptive rainbow-slick surface of Joan Didion's third novel is due in large part to the voice of her narrator.

But what are we to make of Didion's choice of title? Why call this most secular of stories *A Book of Common Prayer*? Having created a surrogate author in the form of Grace, the real author has greatly limited the ways in which she can speak in her own person. One of the few possibilities left is a suggestive title. At one point she told her editor Henry Robbins that the story was actually Grace's prayer for Charlotte's soul. Although she admits to Sara Davidson that this explanation was "specious," Didion goes on to say, "If you have a narrator, which suddenly I was stuck with, the narrator can't just be telling you a story, something that happened, to entertain you. The narrator has got to be telling you the story for a reason. I think the title probably helped me with that."[7]

The prose of *A Book of Common Prayer* does have a liturgical cadence. The repetition of key phrases and frequent paragraph divisions give Didion's novel a sound and an appearance not unlike that of the Anglican prayer book. The real significance of Didion's title, however, is probably more thematic than formalistic. We know from her review of Cheever's *Falconer* that she considers her background as a white middle-class Episcopalian to be an important influence on her sensibility. Although Didion scarcely mentions religion in her novel, she does concern herself with the plight of characters who are *culturally* white, middle-class, and Protestant. If Marin is sent to an Episcopal day school it is not because her mother is a devout Episcopalian, but because Charlotte is of a certain cultural heritage, because she is the inheritor of no dark or bloodied ground.

The Anglican *Book of Common Prayer* is both the oldest liturgy in the English language and a product of the Protestant Reformation. The services in that book fulfill the ancient function of ritual—they help give a certain order and coherence to our contemplation of spiritual things. (John Crowe Ransom argues that, because ritual is an essential component of human experience, it is necessary to retain a *sense* of ritual even after one has ceased to believe in religious dogma. Accordingly, Didion admits that although she no longer goes to church, she frequently repeats phrases from the prayer book in her mind.[8]) What Joan Didion has given us in *A Book of Common Prayer* is Grace's attempt to find some sense of order and coherence in the life of Charlotte Douglas.

Grace is "witnessing" for Charlotte in much the same way that a believer might witness for her faith. The salient difference, of course, is that Grace has not found order and coherence in Charlotte's life, only chaos and fragmentation; she has not come to rest in a sure faith but remains a confirmed skeptic.

The indefinite article in Didion's title and the fact that her central intelligence is a cancer victim named *Grace* only serve to remind us that this novel lacks an objective system of values, along with a reliable mode of narration. We are still out there where *nothing* is, marvelling at Didion's ability to create aesthetic beauty out of an affirmation of the void. But after the same trick has been turned enough times, one begins to suspect that the void itself is less a sincere reading of the human condition than a necessary environment for the kind of nihilistic parables Didion is so adept at writing. Behind Grace's final self-effacement, one senses an author who is no more comfortable with the despair of the religious agnostic than she is with the certitude of the scientific rationalist. This novel is the common prayer of those who, like Grace and Joan Didion herself, have lost only the power, not the will to believe.

Chapter Eleven

Bananas

When it comes to political wisdom, creative writers tend to be only slightly less self-important than movie stars and rock singers. Shelley may have thought that poets were "the unacknowledged legislators of the world," but for every Harriet Beecher Stowe who changed the course of history, there are hordes of Country Joe McDonalds who can only exhort their followers "to sing louder if you want to end the war." Over the years Joan Didion has generally been a refreshing exception to this rule.

Didion's saving grace as an observer of the political scene has, of course, been her disdain for politics. As a skeptical aristocrat, she has remained outside and above the political fray. Although never a right-wing partisan, she was certainly within her element exposing the political nonsense of the Left during the sixties and seventies. It may have come as a shock to her old colleagues at *National Review*, however, when Didion displayed that same sense of skeptical independence in assessing the Reagan administration's policy toward Latin America. But then, *Salvador* (1983) and *Miami* (1987) are simply additional evidence that editor William F. Buckley was correct when he characterized his journal as "a finishing school for apostates."[1]

Letters from Central America

In reading Didion's *Salvador* one gets the eerie sense that life is imitating art. We remember her telling us in "Why I Write" that the initial inspiration for *A Book of Common Prayer* was the image of the Panama airport at 6:00 A.M. From there it was only a process of extrapolation to make up a country in which to place the airport and a menacing political environment for that country. In *Salvador* Didion takes us back to Boca Grande, even to the point of beginning her account with a description of the El Salvador International Airport. "Most readers will not get very far in this very short book," writes Gene Lyons in *Newsweek*, "without wondering whether she visited this sad and tortured place less to report than to validate the Didion world view."[2]

Whether or not Lyons's rather caustic inference is correct, the turmoil in El Salvador is clearly another instance of the center's not holding, of things falling apart. As one might expect, the brutality of the place is described with the ironic juxtaposition of clinical detail and elegantly cadenced prose that has come to be Didion's trademark. On the fifth page of her text, for example, we read the following: "In El Salvador one learns that vultures go first for the soft tissue, for the eyes, the exposed genitalia, the open mouth. One learns that an open mouth can be used to make a specific point, can be stuffed with something emblematic; stuffed say, with a penis, or, if the point has to do with land title, stuffed with some of the dirt in question. One learns that hair deteriorates less rapidly than flesh, and that a skull surrounded by a perfect corona of hair is a not uncommon sight in the body dumps."[3]

Ironies of situation (what might be termed "found ironies") also abound. We read of young, "barely pubescent" soldiers who "wore crucifixes wrapped with bright yarn, the pink and green of the yarn stained now with dust and sweat"; and of the middle-aged taxi driver wearing expensive sunglasses who at each roadblock "in a motion so abbreviated as to be almost imperceptible, . . . would touch each of the two rosaries that hung from the rearview mirror and cross himself" (*S* 42).

Even in the cities things are seldom what they seem. The Sheraton in Escalon appears festive "with children in the pool and flowers and pretty women in pastel dresses, but there are usually several bullet-proofed Cherokee Chiefs in the parking area, and the men drinking in the lobby often carry the little zippered purses that in San Salvador suggest not passports or credit cards but Browning 9-m.m. pistols" (*S* 23). Still, because the Pipal Indians are no longer flaying each other alive, officials at the American embassy can claim that "from a human-rights point of view, the trend locally is up, or at any rate holding" (*S* 87).

Although Didion spent only two weeks in El Salvador, she conveys a vivid sense of the surface of things (a surface so surrealistic that she "began to see Gabriel Garcia Marquez in a new light, as a social realist" [*S* 59]). El Salvador is a country where many of the major antagonists are from a relatively select group of families. During her stay there Didion became acquainted with Victor Barriere, an artist who was the grandson of General Maxiliano Hernandez Martinez, the dictator of El

Salvador between 1931 and 1944. (A screwball who could have stepped right off the set of Woody Allen's *Bananas,* General Hernandez once tried to halt the spread of smallpox by stringing San Salvador with a web of colored lights.) Victor Barriere remarks on the strangeness of going to school with boys whose fathers his grandfather had ordered shot; however, Didion is discreet enough not to bring up the fact that one of the most active death squads then operating in El Salvador called itself the Maximiliano Hernandez Martinez Brigade. "There are no issues here," a high-placed Salvadoran had told Didion, "only ambitions" (*S* 34).

The "indigenous" culture of El Salvador, like that of Boca Grande, has about it a bogus eclecticism. (Indeed, lifting a phrase from *A Book of Common Prayer,* Didion says of the Indian part of that culture that it "was less remembered than recreated" [*S* 75].) At an exhibition of native crafts in Nahuizalco Didion learns that, although the making of wicker furniture was a traditional native craft, "little of this furniture was now seen because it was hard to obtain wicker in the traditional way. . . . The traditional way of obtaining wicker, it turned out, had been to import it from Guatemala" (*S* 73). Superimposed on the Indian and Catholic cultures of this village were music and dances from other cultural traditions. Blaring from the loudspeakers of the Suprema Beer sound truck were "Roll Out the Barrel," "La Cucaracha," and "Everybody Salsa."

Because of the political activity of the clergy and the violence that routinely takes place in what *norteamericanas* would naively regard as sanctuary, the description of churches becomes an important motif in *Salvador.* In Nahuizalco, Didion notices the absence of men at a mass baptism of thirty or forty babies. ("The reason for this may have been cultural, or may have had to do with the time and the place, and the G-3s [assault rifles] in the schoolyard" [*S* 77].) There are, however, "a few hundred mothers and grandmothers and aunts and godmothers. The altar was decorated with asters in condensed milk cans. The babies fretted, and several of the mothers produced bags of Fritos to quiet them" (*S* 77).

Then there is the Metropolitan Cathedral in San Salvador:

This is the cathedral that the late Archbishop Oscar Arnulfo Romero refused to finish, on the premise that the work of the Church took precedence over its display, and the high walls of raw concrete bristle with structural rods, rusting now, staining the concrete, sticking out at wrenched and violent angles. The wiring is exposed. Fluorescent tubes hang askew. The great high altar is backed by warped plyboard. The cross on the altar is of bare incandescent bulbs, but the bulbs, that afternoon, were unlit: there was in fact no light at all on the main altar, no light on the cross, no light on the globe of the world that showed the northern American continent in gray and the southern in white; no light on the dove above the globe, *Salvador del Mundo.* (*S* 78–79)

If the strife in El Salvador were simply a civil war involving local interests, it is doubtful that Joan Didion would have written a book about it. What interests Americans about El Salvador and what accounts for Didion's presence there is our own government's increasing commitment to preventing yet another strategically located Latin American country from falling into Communist hands. Consequently, the influence of the United States in El Salvador is pervasive. Didion's practiced journalistic eye tends to focus on small but telling evidences of this influence. She tells us, for example, of the Senorita El Salvador contest (part of the Senorita Universo contest) in which "a local entertainer wearing a white dinner jacket and a claret-colored bow tie sang 'The Impossible Dream,' in Spanish" (*S* 58). When an earthquake damaged much of San Salvador, an emergency generator quickly got things jumping again at the discotheque off the lobby of the Hotel Camino Real, where "waiters in black cowboy hats darted about the dance floor carrying drinks, and dancing continued, to Jerry Lee Lewis's 'Great Balls of Fire' " (*S* 61).

In an era when Buddhist monks and protestors against domestic unemployment will set themselves on fire for television cameras and political demonstrations of all stripes seem to exist primarily because "the whole world is watching," it is not surprising that the outside media both covers and helps to shape events in El Salvador. At one point Didion notes that when the Falklands war eclipsed public interest in the Central American conflict, the Hotel Camino Real discontinued its breakfast buffet and the networks stopped sending down movies (*Apocalypse Now* and Woody Allen's *Bananas*) for their reporters to show at midnight on their video recorders. In an event that must have happened because Didion would not have dared to invent it, a Danish film crew on location in Haiti and El Salvador shoots a movie about a foreign correspondent who, in one scene, actually interviews Roberto D'Aubuisson on camera. The crew "left San Salvador without making it entirely clear whether or not they had ever told D'Aubuisson it was just a movie" (*S* 51).

John Gregory Dunne has said that as a screenwriter his most instructive experiences have been watching the bad movies of good directors because "in each there is a moment or sequence that stands out in such bold relief from the surrounding debris as to make the reasons for its effectiveness clear."[4] The same is surely true of literature. Although *Salvador* is not really a "bad book," it is one of Didion's least effective efforts. It seems to me that Didion writes her best journalism when she is able to establish a personal connection with a place, as in her elegiac essays about Northern California, or when she is discovering the inherent literary qualities of a public phenomenon, as in her rendering of the Lucille Miller story and her deflation of the buffoonish Bishop Pike. In *Salvador,* neither is the case.

Because her stay in El Salvador was brief and exclusively professional, Didion has no personal stake in that embattled land. Many of her individual descriptions border on brilliance, but the closest she comes to finding a *character* who excites her literary interest are her brief encounters with American ambassador Deane Hinton. As a cosmopolitan man with western American roots, Hinton seems to be Didion's kind of guy. In his presence she is even able to believe, if only for a moment, that "the American undertaking in El Salvador might turn out to be, from the right angle, in the right light, just another difficult but possible mission in another troubled but possible country" (*S* 87–88).

Although Didion studiously avoids partisan polemics, the political message of her book, beginning with the opening epigraph (from Conrad's *Heart of Darkness*) and running to the final page, is clear: El Salvador is a Third World backwater that cannot be salvaged for U.S. interests, and to take one side or the other there is to fall prey to the sort of self-delusion that afflicted Conrad's Kurtz. Predictably, Ronald Reagan is Didion's Mistah Kurtz. Early in the book, she watches Reagan and Doris Day cavort on Salvadoran television in *The Winning Team,* a 1952 Warner Brothers movie about the baseball pitcher Grover Cleveland Alexander. Then, at the end of the narrative, we see the Great Communicator "certifying" El Salvador's progress toward political stability and human rights, even as the carnage and repression continue. The first of these scenes is simply a variation on all the tired Bonzo jokes that have plagued Reagan for most of his political career. The second, however, raises a far more substantive issue.

At the time of Didion's visit to El Salvador, it was clear to most objective observers that the government of that country was unable to stop the terrorists on the Left and unwilling to stop those on the Right. Thus, disingenuous assurances of progress on human rights seemed slightly surrealistic, as if one were talking about adherence to the Weight Watchers diet (you really can't expect these people to stop murdering each other cold turkey, can you?). The certification charade, however, begs an important question in assuming that strategic self-interest is an insufficiently moral basis for a nation's foreign policy.

If the salient issue in El Salvador is whether the United States can impose *norteamericana* democracy on that troubled land, then Didion's fashionably isolationist sentiments are certainly compelling. Yet reasonable persons might argue that U.S. national security is better served if our thugs rather than Castro's are in charge in Central America. Didion rather cavalierly dismisses that consideration by observing, "no one could doubt that Cuba and Nicaragua had at various points supported the armed opposition to the Salvadoran government, but neither could anyone be surprised by this" (*S* 94). What she does not say is that the reason no one could be surprised by this is that the Left produces its own Kurtzes. Fidel may never have played Grover Cleveland Alexander, but he was a mediocre minor league pitcher before becoming the Robespierre of Cuba.

In *Salvador* we have something like the story of Charlotte Douglas, the *norteamericana* who lives for a time in a strife-torn Hispanic police state, regards herself as *una turista,* and tries unsuccessfully to sell her vision of reality to the *New Yorker* in a series of "Letters from Central America." *Salvador* is essentially Joan Didion's "Letters from Central America," published originally not in the *New Yorker,* but in the *New York Review of Books.* In reading these letters, one cannot help remembering that at the end of *A Book of Common Prayer,* Grace concedes: "I am less and less certain that this story has been one of delusion."
"Unless the delusion was mine" (*BCP*).[5]

A Tale of Two Cities

Robert Frost once said that he was a conservative in his youth so he could afford to be a radical in his old age. While this is not entirely the case with Joan Didion, her political consciousness seems to have been raised to a higher level during the Reagan years than at any earlier point in her life. The woman who was once proud to have been a member of the apolitical "silent generation" told a reporter for *Vanity Fair* in the fall of 1987 that she was "irritated that so many people have found it

easy to overlook what's going on, to live in the comfort zone."[6] In this
instance "what's going on" is the policy of the six U.S. administrations
toward Latin America and the various domestic ramifications thereof.
From the Bay of Pigs to the Iran-Contra scandal, policymakers in
Washington have had to extricate themselves from the mess created by
their awkward attempts to apply the Monroe Doctrine in a nuclear age.
It has been, in the immortal words of Allen Dulles, a massive "disposal
problem."

These words were spoken by Dulles, who was head of the CIA, to
President John F. Kennedy in reference to aborting the Bay of Pigs
invasion and thereby "cutting loose what the CIA knew to be a vengeful
asset"[7]—the Cuban exiles manning that invasion. According to court
historian Arthur M. Schlesinger, Jr., President Kennedy's response was
to say: "If we have to get rid of these 800 men, it is much better to
dump them in Cuba than in the United States, especially if that is
where they want to go." Although Didion does not believe that Schlesinger has much of an ear for dialogue and points out that the eventual
invasion force was closer to 1,500 than to 800, she finds "dump them
in Cuba" and "disposal problem" to be lines with an authentic ring to
them. Nevertheless, she admits that "only after I had spent time in
Miami did I begin to see them as curtain lines, or as the cannon which
the protagonist brings onstage in the first act so that it may be fired
against him in the third" (M 83).

At one level, Didion's 1987 book *Miami* is an extended feature story
on the exile community that fled Castro's reign of terror in the early
sixties and came to dominate the politics and economy of America's
most Caribbean city. As we can see, however, Didion's real concern is
not with immigrant sociology but with the baroque political entangle-
ments of Miami and Washington, D.C. It is a tale of two cities set in
what the Cubans would regard as primarily the worst of times. Although Didion does not endorse a second Bay of Pigs landing (nor the
first one for that matter), she is much more sympathetic to the Cuban
patriots than to the cynical politicians in Washington who have manipulated and exploited them for twenty-five years.

If Teddy Roosevelt's policy toward Cuba, and the rest of the world,
was to speak softly but carry a big stick, the Kennedy and Reagan
administrations (and, to a lesser extent, those that came in between)
were content to talk tough while stopping short of an actual confronta-
tion with Soviet imperialism in his hemisphere. Unfortunately, the
Cuban exiles and their more militant allies insisted on a literal interpre-

tation of Washington's anti-Communist rhetoric and felt betrayed when there was no action behind the brave words. Instead of receiving support they found themselves set up to play the role of right-wing terrorists. As one prominent Cuban nationalist, the Miami architect Raul Rodriguez, pointed out to Didion at supper one night: "Cuba never grew plastique. Cuba grew tobacco. Cuba grew sugarcane. Cuba never grew C-4 [explosives]. . . . C-4, Raul Rodriguez said, and he slammed his palm down on the white tablecloth as he said it, grew here" (*M* 163).

The two principal reactions of Miami's Anglo minority (and much of the rest of the nation) to the Cuban exiles have been condescension and nativist rancor. The first was epitomized in a column George Will wrote for *Newsweek* under the title "Miami Nice." Will cited the Cuban experience as "a new installment in the saga of America's absorptive capacity" and recalled the seven Cubans who had been gotten together to brief him as "exemplary Americans," who "initiated a columnist to fried bananas and black-bean soup and other Cuban contributions to the tanginess of American life" (see *M* 60). To Didion's mind, such attitudes represent "a particularly gringo fantasy, one in which Miami Cubans, who came from a culture which had represented western civilization in this hemisphere since before there was a United States of America, appeared exclusively as vendors of plantains, their native music 'pulsing' behind them" (*M* 61).

The nativist response to increasing Cuban domination of Miami often manifests itself in a testiness about the ubiquity of Spanish. A reporter for the *Miami Herald,* for example, complained that when he called the listed phone number of one of the Cuban candidates for mayor, neither of the two women he spoke to knew enough English to tell him whether or not this was the candidate's house. What surprises Didion is not that the reporter was spoken to in Spanish but that he seemed incapable of saying, "*Es la casa de Raul Masvidal?*"; to which the likely response would have been "*Sí*" or "*No.*" To her the story of this call "appeared not as a statement of literal fact but as shorthand, a glove thrown down, a stand, a cry from the heart of a beleagured raj" (*M* 67). In 1980, the year of the Mariel boatlift, bumper stickers started appearing around town that said: "WILL THE LAST AMERICAN TO LEAVE MIAMI PLEASE BRING THE FLAG" (*M* 67).

That Didion should view the Cuban exiles as sympathetically as she does might come as a surprise to those who remember what the California gentry of *Run River* thought about "wetbacks." If anything, she seems to admire the sense of community that makes the exiles, rich and poor, a single people. If the cohesive force holding them together is the improbable dream of returning to a non-Communist Cuba, Didion knows enough about doomed commitments not to patronize those who cling to them. (It is only when she spots a poseur or publicity hound that her satire moves into overdrive.) When she describes an immigrant rally, it is with a clear and nonpatronizing eye: "There were National Rifle Association windbreakers and there were T-shirts featuring the American flag and the legend "THESE COLORS DON'T RUN" and there were crucifixes on bare skin and there were knife sheaths on belts slung so low that Jockey shorts showed, but there were also Brooks Brothers shirts, and rep ties, and briefcases of supple leather" (*M* 16–17).

The reader who comes to Didion's *Miami* looking for specific policy recommendations is likely to be disappointed. Despite her sympathy for the Cuban exiles, she is not about to urge Washington to back their counterrevolution and seems to be almost as scornful of the hard-line right-wingers who do so as she is of the cynical pragmatists who simply milk the situation for their partisan advantage. Ronald Reagan comes across as a man whose heart is with the activists and head is with the pragmatists. (Although Didion does not say so, it is precisely this sort of ambivalence that allowed the president to call Oliver North "an American hero" on the same day that he accepted North's resignation.) Those who listen to the chief executive only when his heart is speaking run the risk of transforming themselves from brave freedom fighters into a disposal problem. Perhaps a candid admission that the United States is not prepared to wage war in this hemisphere would be preferable to all the bluster and saber rattling. But in foreign policy, being honest is simply a means of reducing one's strategic leverage. To keep the bad guys guessing in frustration, it is sometimes necessary to keep the good ones hoping in vain.

Of course, one does not read Joan Didion primarily for her sociological or political insight, as acute as those may be at times, but for her amazing facility with language. One opens a book by Didion expecting to find a prose that is elegant, precise, witty, and cadenced. Unfortunately, *Miami* disappoints more often than it delivers. Perhaps attempting to write in a manner appropriate to her convoluted subject matter (political intrigue and the like), she sounds too often like a cut-rate Henry James. It is not particularly difficult to navigate her heavily subordinated sentences, but the sound is too often flat.

Fortunately, *Miami* contains enough remnants of Didion at her best to suggest that she has simply misplaced rather than lost her marvelous sense of the absurd. For example, early in the book, she writes:

Inside the autopsy room the hands of the two young men were encased in the brown paper bags which indicated that the police had not yet taken what they needed for laboratory studies. Their flesh had the marbelized yellow look of the recently dead. There were other bodies in the room, in various stages of autopsy, and a young woman in a white coat taking eyes, for the eye bank. "Who are we going to start on next?" one of the assistant medical examiners was saying. "The fat guy? Let's do the fat guy." (*M* 35)

The foreign policy implicitly endorsed by *Miami* is no different from the one found in *Salvador*—a skeptical isolationism based on the assumption that no good can come from American meddling in the affairs of other countries. To the extent that anyone actually believes that our government is interested only in making the world (or the hemisphere) safe for democracy, such skepticism is well founded. In terms of the quality of life enjoyed by the Cuban people, the difference between living under a right-wing authoritarian regime and a left-wing totalitarian one probably does not justify the blood and treasure necessary to replace the latter with the former. (Strategic self-interest, of course, is another matter.) Whether it is her own particular version of ethnocentricity or simply hard-headed realism, Didion seems incapable of envisioning Latin American politics devoid of corruption, intrigue, bloodshed, and massive instability.

This point is best illustrated by Didion's description of Carlos Prio, president of Cuba from 1948 to 1952 and a resident of Miami for the last twenty-five years of his life. " 'They say that I was a terrible president of Cuba,' Carlos Prio once said to Arthur M. Schlesinger, Jr., during a visit to the Kennedy White House some ten years into the quarter-century Miami epilogue to his four-year Havana presidency. 'That may be true. But I was the best president Cuba ever had' " (*M* 12).

Chapter Twelve
Pacific Distances

Next to her home state of California, the place that has probably had the most persistent hold on Joan Didion's imagination is the farther western frontier of Hawaii. (In her home in Los Angeles she always keeps one clock set to Honolulu time.[1]) From her second professional publication, a review of James Michener's *Hawaii* in the 5 December 1959 issue of the *National Review,* to her 1984 novel *Democracy,* Didion has written repeatedly about her fascination with our fiftieth state—not as an exotic island paradise, but as an integral, if idiosyncratic, part of the larger American scene.

In *Slouching Towards Bethlehem* she tells us that she has always thought of Hawaii as three places. Most recently, it has come to be a vacation resort, "a big rock candy mountain in the Pacific which presented itself . . . in newspaper photographs of well-fed Lincoln-Mercury dealers relaxing beside an outrigger at the Royal Hawaiian Hotel" (*STB* 189). This Hawaii was itself made possible by World War II, a conflict America entered because of the Japanese attack on its Hawaiian naval base. Going back even further, Didion notes that the Hawaii of Pearl Harbor was preceded by a feudal society that exists today only in memory as a region of Chekhovian doom. It was "a place which seemed to have to do neither with war nor with vacationing godmothers but only with the past, and with loss" (*STB* 189). Joan Didion has written movingly about all three Hawaiis.

West of Eden

For many years Didion associated the vacationland Hawaii with a pink palace in the sand known as the Royal Hawaiian Hotel. From the time that it was built in 1927 until well after World War II the Royal was the Pacific playground for the aristocracy of the mainland. In 1970 Didion observed that anyone behind the roped enclosure that defined the Royal's private beach could assume that others behind the rope would "know people we know." It was "an enclave of apparent strangers ever on the verge of discovering that their nieces roomed in Lagunita at Stanford the same year, or that their best friends lunched together during the last Crosby." ("The fact that anyone behind the rope would understand the word 'Crosby' to signify a golf tournament at Pebble Beach suggests the extent to which the Royal Hawaiian is not merely a hotel but a social idea, one of the few extant clues to a certain kind of American life" [*WA* 13].)

Because Didion was herself a frequent visitor to the Royal, she could speak of its patrons in the first-person plural. Although the hint of snobbery is inescapable, it is tempered by the realization that the social idea embodied by the Royal is anachronistic and, hence, slightly ridiculous. Didion contends that "what the place reflected in the Thirties it reflects still, in less flamboyant mutations: a kind of life lived on the streets where the oldest trees grow" (*WA* 139). Consequently, it is a life largely undisturbed by the convulsions of the larger society. On the day after Robert Kennedy was shot, Didion stood at the Royal's newsstand, where the California papers arrive one—sometimes two—days late, and overheard a man and his wife commenting on the heavy early turnout for the California primary. "Later in the morning," she tells us, "I overheard this woman discussing the assassination: her husband had heard the news when he dropped by a brokerage office to get the day's New York closings" (*WA* 139–40).

One can easily imagine the Northern California gentry of Didion's childhood vacationing at the Royal Hawaiian. But as we know from *Run River* and *Slouching Towards Bethlehem,* that class of people has become as moribund as the Compsons and Sartorises of the Faulknerian South. It is therefore not surprising that when the Sheraton built a large hotel on the grounds of the Royal Hawaiian, Didion and Dunne switched their allegiance to the Kahala Hilton, the embodiment of a social idea much more representative of the jacuzzi culture of present-day Southern California. Didion's account of life at the Kahala is appropriately titled "Where *Tonight Show* Guests Go to Rest."

"The last time I visited the Kahala Hilton in Honolulu," she writes, "Rod Stewart was there, just off the road, and Helen Reddy was there, just off the road. Carol Burnett had recently come and gone, as had the queen of England. Totie Fields and Steve and Eydie Lawrence and Cher and Chastity Bono had also come and gone, but Joe Frazier was there, and the day he flew out Muhammad Ali arrived."[2] The Kahala is a place where the big news during a particular week is that the president of CBS has been deposed, or—as it is cryptically recounted among the initiated—that "Bob Wood is out." To have known or to have inferred this news a week or even a few days before it happened is considered a mark of status at the Kahala. (It is probably to Didion's credit that she had to be told who Bob Wood was.) The point would seem to be that the entertainment capitals of New York, Hollywood, and Las Vegas are less physical locations than floating metonymies. The *Tonight Show,* like Hemingway's Paris, is a moveable feast.

If Didion's sketches of the Royal Hawaiian and the Kahala Hilton are admittedly lightweight feature journalism, her meditations on wartime Hawaii contain some of her best writing. Because she was already seven years old when the attack on Pearl Harbor occurred, it remains a vivid memory. When someone four years younger than Didion chided her for being so moved by the sight of a sunken ship at Pearl Harbor and insisted that the assassination of John Kennedy was "the single most indelible event of what he kept calling 'our generation' " (*STB* 193), she could tell him only that they belonged to different generations; she was at a loss to explain her true feelings. In an essay entitled "Letter from Paradise, 21° 19′ N., 157° 52′ W." she belatedly attempts to do just that.

Didion's account of her feelings about Pearl Harbor includes, without comment, an excerpt from a January 1941 issue of *Vogue.* Here, John W. Vandercock describes Hawaii as "*our Gibralter.*" Pearl Harbor, we are told, is "*the one sure sanctuary in the whole of the vast Pacific both for ships and men*" (*STB* 191). The implication, which is so obvious that it need not be stated, is that the attack on Pearl Harbor was a severe blow to American hubris. Didion responds, however, not in condescension but in sorrow. For her the Hawaii of Pearl Harbor is best memorialized not in the countless movies watched by children too young to remember the real event or in the souvenir shops that sell the "Picture Story of December 7." Rather, it is to be found in the gray harbor water around what is still visible of the *Arizona:* "the rusted after-gun turret breaking the gray water, the flag at full mast because the Navy considers the Arizona still in commission, a full crew aboard, 1,102 men from forty-nine states" (*STB* 192). And preeminently it is to be found in the cemetery called Punchbowl. "They all seem to be twenty years old, the boys buried up there," Didion tells us, ". . . twenty and nineteen and eighteen and sometimes not that old" (*STB* 193). One marine—Samuel Foster Harmon—died at Iwo Jima, fifteen days short of his seventeenth birthday.

If the Hawaii of war is the one that most moves Joan Didion, feudal

Hawaii is probably the one that most intrigues her. Whatever it may have been in reality, it is clear that she imagines it to have been an agrarian aristocracy not unlike that of the antebellum South or pre–World War II Sacramento. In "Letter from Paradise" she suggests that that Hawaii fell victim to the industrial development launched by auto magnate Henry J. Kaiser, a sort of mid-Pacific Flem Snopes. "My aunt married into a family which had lived for generations in the Islands," she writes, "but they did not even visit there any more; 'Not since Mr. *Kaiser*,' they would say, as if the construction of the Hawaiian Village Hotel on a few acres of reclaimed tidal flat near Fort De Russy had in one swing of the builder's crane wiped out their childhoods and their parents' childhoods, blighted forever some sub-tropical cherry orchard where every night in the soft blur of memory the table was set for forty-eight in case someone dropped by" (*STB* 189–90).

In a sense World War II helped bring Hawaii into the mainstream of American life. The paradise remembered so fondly by Didion's aunt's family was a regressive oligarchy actually destroyed more by postwar prosperity than by Henry Kaiser. Since relatively few Hawaiians benefited from this older arrangement, it is understandable that they shed few tears over its demise. (The same was of course true, though on a smaller scale, of Didion's native California.) If pre–World War II Hawaii was a highly isolated and atypical part of America, it was nevertheless subject to some of the same social dynamics as the rest of the nation. Perhaps those dynamics are best understood by an American of western origins, who can say, "I sat as a child on California beaches and imagined that I saw Hawaii, a certain shimmer in the sunset, a barely perceptible irregularity glimpsed intermittently through squinted eyes" (*STB* 188).

The Education of Inez Victor

At the time that *A Book of Common Prayer* was published, Didion announced that she was working on a novel set in Hawaii. In the spring of 1984 that long-awaited Hawaiian novel finally appeared. In the process of composition, however, the book had come to be no more *about* Hawaii than *Play It as It Lays* is about Hollywood or *A Book of Common Prayer* about Central America. The fact that Didion changed her title from *Pacific Distances* to *Democracy* suggests that Hawaii is finally less an essential setting for her story than a useful backdrop against which to depict American life (or at least that part of it she knows best) in the mid-1970s.

The protagonist of *Democracy*, Inez Christian Victor, is the daughter of a prominent but decaying Island family and the wife of a liberal California senator who narrowly loses the Democratic presidential nomination in 1972. The love of her life, however, is a shadowy "information specialist" who operates on the fringes of the CIA. She follows him to Southeast Asia on the eve of the fall of Vietnam (to retrieve her daughter—a heroin addict who has drifted to Saigon because she hears that employment opportunities are good there) and sees him drown in a hotel pool in Jakarta. She brings the body back to Hawaii to be buried under a jacaranda tree at Schofield barracks and returns to Kuala Lampur to work with refugees. Somewhat on the periphery of this story is the public chaos of Indochina and the more local calamity of the murder of Inez's sister and her apparent lover (a Nisei congressman) by Inez's father. Choosing to make neither history nor domestic tragedy the focus of her novel, Didion gives us instead a brilliant comedy of political manners that blossoms into a strangely compelling romance.

Because the brunt of Didion's satire is borne by fatuous New Age liberals and her most admirable character is what one such liberal (Inez's husband, Harry) calls a "war lover," *Democrary* has resulted in Didion's being at least partially restored to the good graces of those conservative literati who had placed *Salvador* on their index of forbidden books. Indeed, George Will went so far as to compare *Democracy* to Henry James's *The Bostonians,* saying that Harry Victor, "like James's reformer, has no inner life other than a catalog of his public sympathies."[3] From a considerably different point on the political spectrum, Mary McCarthy writes: "At times Harry Victor seems meant to recall one of the Kennedys (most likely Bobby) or all of them. There is a hint of Jack's womanizing, and the suggestion that Inez Victor may have a 'drinking problem' brings to mind Teddy and Joan."[4] What is clear to both Will and McCarthy is that in the life lived by the Harry Victors of this world, politics and celebrity are ultimately indistinguishable.

Among the women who share a passion for both the ideology and the body of Harry Victor are the rock singer Connie Willis and the political aide Frances Landau. "Both women," Didion tells us, "were just alike. They listened to Harry the same way. They had the same way of deprecating their own claims to be heard." For Connie Willis this meant saying about her singing, "I just do two lines of coke and scream." For Frances Landau it means saying of her considerable wealth, "It's just a means to an end."[5] Frances, whom Harry introduces as "a grandniece of the first Jew on the Supreme Court of the United

States," is so devoted to Harry that she listens to everything he says "with studied attention, breaking her gaze only to provide glosses for the less attentive, her slightly hyperthyroid face sharp in the candle-light and her voice intense, definite, an insistent echo of every opinion she had ever heard expressed" (D 82). In contrast, when Inez Victor flew back to New York on the press plane after Harry had conceded the 1972 California primary, she was reported to have sung " 'It's All Over Now, Baby Blue' with an ABC cameraman and a photographer from *Rolling Stone*" (D 49).

In combining the wimpish superficiality of Leonard Douglas with the egocentric nastiness of Warren Bogart, Harry Victor may be Didion's least attractive male character. With her unerring sense of language, Didion allows Victor to condemn himself with his own clichés. He is the author of such memorable tracts as "Justice for Whom—A Young Lawyer Wants Out" and *The View from the Streets: Root Causes, Radical Solutions and a Modest Proposal;* when he makes a human rights junket to a Third World trouble spot, he refers to the anarchy and bloodshed as "the normal turbulence of a nascent democracy" (D 103); and in describing "the most socially responsible generation ever to hit American campuses," he gushes, "Admiration, Christ no, what I feel when I see you guys is a kind of awe" (D 62). After leaving the Senate, Harry establishes a public-spirited organization called the Alliance for Democratic Institutions and frequently invokes the name of the pre-miere Democrat. "You talk down to the American people at your peril," he says. "Either Jefferson was right or he wasn't. . . . I happen to believe he was" (D 57). The audience on this occasion is a physicist who Harry claims "hadn't done his homework." ("Those guys get their Nobels and start coasting" [D 58].)

Harry and Inez are the parents of twin children named Jessica and Adlai. Although Mary McCarthy may be right in seeing a suggestion of the Kennedy curse in Jessie Victor's teenage drug habit, Didion is quick to point out that "Jessie never thought of herself as a problem. She never considered her use of heroin as an act of rebellion, or a way of life, or even a bad habit of particular remark; she considered it a consumer decision. Jessie Victor used heroin simply because she pre-ferred heroin to coffee, aspirin, and cigarettes, as well as to movies, records, cosmetics, clothes, and lunch" (D 172).

Jessie's even more dimwitted brother is enrolled in a Boston area college "accredited for draft deferment" (D 62), talks about being in school "in Cambridge" to suggest that he is a Harvard man, and orders dinner by asking for "a shrimp cocktail and the New York stripper, medium bloody, sour cream and chives on the spud" (*D* 175). When his mother suggests that he go to the hospital to see a girl whom he has almost killed in a car wreck (another Kennedy allusion?), Adlai says, "She's definitely on the agenda" (*D* 62). And when the family is trying to figure out why Jessie has left her job as a waitress in Seattle to look for work in Vietnam, he says, "Maybe she heard she could score there" (*D* 177).

Like the uprooted women in Didion's earlier novels, Inez Christian Victor is a long way from the home of her youth. The glimpses we get of that home (or to be more accurate, what has become of it) suggest something about the "Hawaiian novel" Didion might have written. "Imagine my mother dancing," that novel was to have begun. Then it was changed to the third person: "Inez imagined her mother dancing"; or perhaps: "Inez remembered her mother dancing" (*D* 21). "What I had there," Didion tells us, "was a study in provincial manners, in the acute tyrannies of class and privilege by which people assert themselves against the tropics" (*D* 22). But that world was too remote to Didion to accommodate itself to the scope of a novel.

As the social dynamic of Honolulu changed, various members of the Christian family either deserted the Islands for the mainland (as Inez and her mother, Carol Christian, did) or lost their minds in the trauma of social change (as Inez's father, Paul Christian, did). By the mid-1970s the major power in the Christian family had shifted to Uncle Dwight, whose assertion of that family's pride can be seen in his planning the funeral of his niece (murdered by her own father). "Just the regular service in and out," he says, "the ashes to ashes business. And maybe a couple of what do you call them, psalms. Not the one about the Lord is my goddamn shepherd. . . . Passive crap, the Lord is my shepherd. . . . No sheep in this family" (*D* 157).

The circumstances of the murder of Inez's sister Janet Christian Ziegler by their father are left shrouded in ambiguity. We know that at the time of the shooting Janet was entertaining a Nisei congressman named Wendall Omura and that Paul Christian had earlier written the Honolulu *Advertiser* demanding " 'retraction' of a photograph showing Janet presenting an Outdoor Circle Environmental Protection Award for Special Effort in Blocking Development to Rep. Wendell Omura," and had concluded his complaint with the enigmatic phrase "lest we forget" (*D* 135). The hint of an interracial affair and the conflict of cultures remains vague precisely because it is filtered through the prism of Paul Christian's insanity. What is not vague is Didion's rendering of that insanity itself.

Not only did Paul Christian write letters to newspapers demanding the "retraction" of offensive photographs, but he made a point of telling people that he lived in a single room at the YMCA and was reduced to eating canned tuna. (That he actually was not reduced to such circumstances and that canned tuna was not particularly cheap did not dissuade him from camping the role of the "impoverished noble" [*D* 131].) Moreover, Paul Christian had the habit of giving Inez's number to strangers he met on airplanes and then calling "to remonstrate with her when he heard that she had been short on the telephone. 'I think you might have spared ten minutes,' Paul Christian had said on one such call. 'This young man you hung up on happens to have a quite interesting grassy-knoll slant on Sal Mineo's murder, he very much wanted Harry to hear it' " (*D* 66).

When people say "have a nice day" to him, Paul Christian replies, "sorry I've made other plans." When Inez visits him in jail after the double murder, he wants to talk not about his immediate troubles but about who has Leilani Taylor's koa settee (Inez does, in the house in Amagansatt). He still calls the freestyle the Australian crawl and can hum a few bars of "The Darktown Strutters Ball." The only two extant photographs of Paul Christian show him, first, playing backgammon with John Huston in Cuernavaca in 1948, and second, leaving the Honolulu YMCA in handcuffs in 1975. In both he is barefoot, but in the second his cuffed hands are "raised above his head in a posture of theatrical submission, even crucifixion. . . . VICTOR FAMILY TOUCHED BY ISLAND TRAGEDY, the caption read in *The New York Times*" (*D* 29).

Given Didion's feel for that mid-Pacific cherry orchard that was feudal Hawaii, it is surprising that her "Hawaiian novel" is concerned only peripherally with the social reality of our fiftieth state. In its own way, however, *Democracy* is as much a novel about the American West as anything Joan Didion has ever written. In it Hawaii becomes a way station on the road to America's ultimate western frontier—Southeast Asia. (In "Letter from Paradise" Didion speaks of sailors who got drunk in Honolulu because "they were no longer in Des Moines and not yet in Da Nang" [*STB* 195].) As Walt Whitman proclaimed over a century ago, the rondure of the Earth leads us not to some apocalyptic West but back east from whence we came. America's manifest destiny, however, has not even produced a mystical passage to India, but helicopters lifting off the roof of the embassy in Saigon during the final days of the only war the United States has ever lost.

If *Democracy* is finally more about Vietnam than Hawaii, Didion hardly pretends to speak the definitive word on that watershed in the history of American vanity. What she does give us in the fall of Saigon is another vivid image of things falling apart, of a culture vexed to nightmare. But it is an image untainted by tendentious political moralizing. To the extent that there is any political temperament informing this novel, it is probably conservative in the skeptical, antiutopian sense of the term. In the last analysis, ideology is less important to Didion than individual character. It is not the liberal humanist Harry but Jack Lovett, the man he has labeled a "war lover," who possesses a sufficient sense of responsibility to accompany Inez to Vietnam to rescue the drug-addicted Jessie from the ruins of a crusade spawned by liberal self-delusion. (Like Tom and Daisy Buchanan, Harry Victor is a careless man who allows others to clean up the mess that he has made.) Jack even succeeds in enticing Jessie into his custody by promising to take her to a John Wayne movie.

If Harry Victor is the most contemptible male character in Didion's fiction, Jack Lovett is probably the most admirable. He is a man who combines vitality and realism with compassion and sentiment. He may even be a closet romantic, a latter-day Rhett Butler. (There is perhaps a bit of the coquettish Miss Scarlett in Inez, who, when introducing Jack to her co-workers at *Vogue,* says: "He can't stay. . . . Because he's running a little coup somewhere. I just bet" [*D* 34].) As the professional rogue with the heart of gold and an unrequited passion, Jack Lovett is not only more attractive but also more interesting than the numbingly predictable Harry Victor. The contradictions he embodies are suggested early in the novel when Didion tells us about a UPI photographer who had run into Jack in a Hong Kong restaurant where the customers brought their own bottles with their names taped to the outside. Jack Lovett's bottle, a quart of Johnnie Walker Black, bears the name "J. LOCKHART." " 'You don't want your name on too many bottles around town,' Jack Lovett reportedly said when the photographer mentioned the tape on the label." "This was a man," Didion reminds us, "who for more than twenty years had maintained a grave attraction to a woman whose every move was photographed" (*D* 41).

By the end of the novel Jack Lovett is dead, and Inez—like all the Didion women who have preceded her—is alone. Her husband and children essentially lost to her and her childhood home destroyed by a bizarre "Island tragedy," Inez vows to stay on the last Pacific frontier and care for the living casualties of war, "until the last refugee was dispatched," something that Didion thinks is unlikely to happen in "Inez's or my lifetime" (*D* 234). Her stance reflects neither liberal sentimentality nor conservative obligation so much as Christian charity. As Mary McCarthy has noted, Inez makes "the choice of Guinevere: to take the veil. Kuala Lampur is her Almesbury."[6] When all external frontiers have been traversed, the only remaining refuge is the West within. In one particularly evocative passage Inez describes "the Singapore Airlines flight that leaves Honolulu at 3:45 A.M. and at 9:40 A.M. one day later lands at Kai Tak Hong Kong" as "an eleven-hour dawn . . . , exactly the way she hoped dying would be" (*D* 188).

In this imagistic, elliptical novel much is left to conjecture. More than in any of her previous works, Didion has helped to fuel this conjecture by an almost compulsive literary allusiveness. Not only is the Hemingway iceberg technique working overtime, but we hear echoes of certain writers and come across references—both direct and oblique—to a host of others. On the first two pages of Chapter 11 alone the names of George Orwell, Ernest Hemingway, Henry Adams, Norman Mailer, A. E. Housman, T. S. Eliot, and Delmore Schwartz are invoked (not to mention a favorite of composition textbook authors— one "Joan Didion"). Here Didion reminisces about a class she taught at Berkeley on "the idea of democracy in the work of certain post-industrial writers" (*D* 71). This and the reference to Henry Adams draw our attention to the fact that Didion has given her book the same title as Adams's 1880 novel—*Democracy*.

Although Mary McCarthy admits to making nothing of the two novels' having the same name, Thomas R. Edwards sees both Didion and Adams as displaced aristocrats who with "irony and subtlety confront a chaotic new reality that shatters the orderings of simpler, older ways."[7] It should also be noted that both novels feature female protagonists who have the opportunity to see the workings of our political system up close. The difference is that Adams's Madeleine Lee is a political idealist who becomes disillusioned by what she sees, whereas Didion's Inez is too hardboiled and apolitical ever to have been an idealist. Both women are drawn to strong-willed pragmatists—soldier of fortune Jack Lovett is on the international scene what Adams's wheeler dealer Silas P. Ratcliffe is in domestic politics. Inez, however, is willing to accept Lovett for what he is and loses him only in death, while Madeleine sends Ratcliffe packing when she learns of his true nature. Finally both women, shaken by their experiences in American democracy, leave their native soil for a much older world—Madeleine for Egypt, Inez for Kuala Lampur.

Perhaps an even more suggestive linkage exists between Didion's novel and *The Education of Henry Adams,* particularly the most famous chapter of that book—"The Dynamo and the Virgin." The thesis of this chapter is that over a period of 600 years Western civilization has moved from thirteenth-century unity to nineteenth-century multiplicity, from the age of the Virgin to that of the Dynamo. While this development no doubt represents progress to many, those of a traditionalist sensibility (e.g. Didion, Adams, T. S. Eliot) realize that there is a dark side to progress, that another name for multiplicity is fragmentation.

That we now live in an age when the ultimate fragmentation is prefigured in nuclear fission and that such an age represents an "advance" even beyond the dynamo occurred to Didion when touring Berkeley's nuclear reactor in Etcheverry Hall in 1979. Recalling that experience, she writes:

In my Modern Library copy of *The Education of Henry Adams,* a book I first read and scored at Berkeley in 1954, I see this passage underlined: ". . . to Adams the dynamo became a symbol of infinity. As he grew accustomed to the great gallery of machines"—he is talking about the machines at the 1900 Paris Exposition—"he began to feel the 40-foot dynamos as a moral force, much as the early Christians felt the Cross." After I had left the TRIGA Mark III reactor in the basement of Etcheverry Hall I wondered for a long time what Henry Adams would have made of the intense blue of the Cerenkov radiation around the fuel rods, the blue past all blue, the blue like light itself, the blue that is actually a shock wave in the pool water and is the exact blue of the glass at Chartres.[8]

To identify the Didion worldview is not the same as saying that *Democracy* is an aesthetically successful embodiment of that worldview. Most commentators have praised Didion's satire and her splendid ear for dialogue, but many feel this novel to be too much a repetition of her earlier work. (As Thomas Mallon notes, "One can sit down with the same syntax too many times, just as one can bump into the same heroine once too often."[9]) What is clearly the most controversial and problematic aspect of *Democracy,* however, is its point of view. Having moved from the selectively limited omniscience of *Run River* to the *director-auteur* stance of *Play It as It Lays* to the Conradian narration of *A*

Book of Common Prayer, Didion takes the further step in *Democracy* of inserting herself as narrator and pretending to be personally acquainted with her characters. Although this device may appear to make Didion's tale a postmodernist novel about novel writing, it also places her in the decidedly premodernist company of George Eliot and William Make-peace Thackeray—both of whom inserted themselves as minor characters in their own fiction.[10] But literary pedigrees aside, what is the point of employing such a technique?

If we accept Didion's own description of the creative process, then her novels begin as images that tell her stories, which she then transcribes. Unfortunately, with this novel, what appeared to be promising images too often led to dead ends. It was not until she saw the image of Inez at the airport in the rain, stepping out from under an umbrella and absently crushing the flowers of her lei against her cheek that Didion found the key that unlocked this novel for her. "This scene," she writes, "is my leper at the door, my Tropical Belt Coal Company, my lone figure on the crest of the immutable hill" (*D* 78).[11] By telling us about the false starts and treating her characters as if they were as real as the figures in her journalism, Didion may be trying to collapse the distinction between fiction and nonfiction narrative. If the new journalism brings the techniques of fiction to the writing of fact, this novel brings the illusion of fact to the writing of fiction. Such a device is for *Democracy* what the title *A Book of Common Prayer* was for Didion's earlier novel—a reason for telling the story. But one suspects that, like Grace Strasser-Mendana, "Joan Didion" has not been the witness she wanted to be.

In the final analysis, there seems to be a transitory and ephemeral quality about Joan Didion's Hawaii. It is a place where celebrities rest their bodies and soldiers bury their dead. It is a place that aristocrats would rather mourn than visit. In reality, it is a place that is coming increasingly to be dominated by its indigenous Oriental population. However, that fourth, most palpable Hawaii seems not to have touched Didion's imagination. Her oft-quoted observation that certain places belong to certain writers was occasioned by the death of James Jones, the novelist whom Didion felt "owned" prewar Hawaii on the strength of his achievement in *From Here to Eternity.* That novel closes on December 7, 1941, the day that Jones's Hawaii ceased to exist as a single imaginative reality. If no subsequent writer has succeeded in capturing what that lost world has become, Joan Didion is one of the few who have cared to try.

Chapter Thirteen

Threescore Miles and Ten

When the first edition of this study appeared in the fall of 1980, Joan Didion's literary reputation was at an all-time high. The publication of *A Book of Common Prayer* had established her credentials as a major contemporary novelist, and the republication of a decade of magazine pieces in *The White Album* simply reminded everyone of what a splendid essayist she was. If there was any controversy over Didion's place in the literary firmament, it had to do with whether her most enduring contributions were in the realm of fiction or nonfiction. In any case, she was regarded by professional reviewers and ordinary readers alike as a remarkably versatile stylist.

Unfortunately, Didion's work in the 1980s has done nothing to enhance her critical stature. Her detractors now feel vindicated, her admirers betrayed, and those who had yet to choose up sides generally perplexed. What this proves, beyond the fact that literary fortunes tend to rise and fall as erratically as the Dow Jones average, is anyone's guess. While it is the purpose of books in this series to resist temporary fashion and concentrate instead on questions of permanent literary merit, that will remain an impossible task as long as human judgment is involved. As for my own judgment, I have been a Joan Didion enthusiast from about the time that *Play It as It Lays* appeared in paperback. Although *Salvador, Democracy,* and *Miami* have not lessened my regard for Didion's talents, these three works have given me a better understanding of their author's peculiar strengths and weaknesses as a writer.

In the realm of fiction, Didion is probably at her best when her technique is least obvious. For this reason, I agree with Joseph Epstein in judging *Run River* to have been her best novel to date. At that early point in her career, Didion was not sophisticated enough to distance herself from her material for fear of being charged with sentimentality. The setting and enveloping action of that novel had the texture of a real story about real people. All that was lacking was the ability to maintain a consistent point of view and to create three-dimensional male characters—qualities Didion would develop in her later work. But by that time she seemed less interested in telling stories than in crafting what amount to extended prose poems on angst.

In describing the first of these prose poems, *Play It as It Lays,* Didion's old teacher Mark Schorer spoke of "a triumph not of insight as such but of style." When reading this novel, Schorer notes, "one thinks of the great *performers* in ballet, opera, and circuses."[1] Like BZ, Didion may be saying that in a world where the substance of things is so nebulous, we are ultimately forced to "fall back on style." But it is a style that is always paying homage to the concept, if not the reality, of moral seriousness. I suspect that those of us who find power and beauty in Didion's work share the feeling D. A. N. Jones experienced upon reading *Play It as It Lays:* of "a certain exhilaration, as when we appreciate a harmonious and well-proportioned painting of some cruelly martryred saint in whom we do not believe."[2]

If *A Book of Common Prayer* brought us back in the direction of a conventional story line, Didion used the persona of Grace to keep that story line at arm's length from both herself and us. If dealt with directly, the most intimate details of Charlotte Douglas's life might have seemed too melodramatic. So we are allowed to glimpse them only through indirection and inference. (Presumably when we witness scenes where Grace was not present, the Conradian technique of imaginative omniscience is at work.) The point is that there is a world of spirit, emotion, and irrationality undreamt of in Grace's philosophy. But to show us that world is to risk bathos, to violate the stiff-upper-lip philosophy that has been one of Hemingway's most baneful legacies to the modern novel.

Although *Democracy* has been panned as probably Didion's least successful novel, it contains some of her best writing. The political satire is brilliant, Harry Victor and Jack Lovett are two of Didion's best drawn male characters, and the image of Hawaii as juncture of East and West is symbolically resonant. If even admirers of this novel are put off by the gimmicky presence of "Joan Didion" as narrator, closer inspection may reveal that what at first glance seemed like a precious gesture of self-indulgence is actually an honest confession of self-doubt. It was the blank spaces and sparse narrative of *Play It as It Lays* and the oblique point of view of *A Book of Common Prayer* that were the tricks. Now the wizard is taking off her mask and conceding that the elegiac Hawaiian novel she wanted to write just wouldn't come. There may be a higher disingenuousness in publishing this self-admitted failure as a "novel," but it will have been well worth the effort if it causes Joan Didion finally to rid herself of "Joan Didion" in all her various aliases and disguises.

The failure of Didion's two most recent nonfiction books to redeem the promise of her earlier work is even easier to explain than is the apparent decline of her novels. As I have suggested earlier, Didion produces her best journalism when she is writing in her own autobiographical voice or when she finds a situation in which life seems to be imitating art. Because she has a novelist's eye for detail, she is also adept at describing places, and her ear for dialogue and finely honed sense of irony have produced some devastatingly funny character sketches. There is a wealth of all of these qualities in both *Slouching Towards Bethlehem* and *The White Album*. What Didion wisely avoids in those two books are the conventional reporting one finds on the front page of a daily newspaper and the sort of punditry that appears on the op-ed page. *Salvador* and *Miami* contain far too much of both.

What distinguishes the "new journalism" from earlier forms of literary nonfiction (feature writing, personal essays, and the like) is its application of the techniques of realistic fiction to the writing of true stories. According to this definition, very few of Didion's pieces (even from the sixties and seventies) really broke new ground. In fact, after we get past "Some Dreamers of the Golden Dream" and "Slouching Towards Bethlehem," what we are left with is a fairly traditional body of work. Even if Didion's stylistic brilliance helped breathe new life into old forms, they still remained old. Thus, it is not all that surprising that when she began writing book-length nonfiction, her approach was more reminiscent of David Halberstam than of Tom Wolfe.

To say this, however, is probably to be unfair to Halberstam. Didion would be the first to admit that she does not possess the gifts of a seasoned reporter, much less of an investigative journalist, and she has never claimed to be an analyst of public policy, only an anthropologist of strange political types. These limitations would not have been particular drawbacks had Didion not tackled subjects that required the talents she so conspicuously lacks. (To have turned *Salvador* and *Miami* into nonfiction novels, such as Hersey's *Hiroshima* or Wolfe's *The Right Stuff*, would have required novelistic technique in addition to, not in place of, the field work of the experienced journalist.) What is good in *Salvador* and *Miami* could have been contained in a couple of feature magazine articles and published with a judicious selection of Didion's previously uncollected prose. In their present form, these two books are embarrassingly *modest* failures.

Joan Didion first made her mark, both in fiction and in journalism, as an interpreter of the sixties. If the seventies and eighties have not provided her with material nearly so promising, the solution may be for her to move backward in time rather than forward. If writers "own" eras as well as places, the time of Didion's life was clearly her youth in postwar Sacramento. (She was able to write as she did about the social fragmentation of the sixties only because her own values were shaped in a much different world.) The cultural transformation that occurred in Northern California during the late forties and early fifties may yet prove to be the mother lode of Didion's muse. No one is better equipped to be the region's Faulkner, or at least its Willa Cather. At her best, Joan Didion writes in a prose as haunting as the memory, many years later, of a childhood summer spent in Vermont—when the ground hardened one night and snow covered the face of an August morning.

Notes and References

Chapter One

1. The first quotation is a blurb from *Esquire* found on the paperback edition of *Run River*. For the second, see John Lahr, "Entrepreneurs of Anxiety," *Horizon*, January 1981, 36, 38–39. This article is a vitriolic attack on Didion and Dunne.

2. See Joseph Epstein, *Plausible Prejudices* (New York: Norton, 1985), 247; and Catherine Stimpson, "The Case of Miss Joan Didion," *Ms.*, January 1973, 36.

3. See Alfred Kazin, "Joan Didion: Portrait of a Professional," *Harper's*, December 1971, 113.

4. *Slouching Towards Bethlehem* (New York: Farrar, Straus & Giroux, 1968), xiv; hereafter cited in the text as *STB*.

5. *The White Album* (New York: Simon & Schuster, 1979), 14; hereafter cited in the text as *WA*.

6. See Katherine Usher Henderson, *Joan Didion* (New York: Ungar, 1981), 3.

7. "American Summer," *Vogue*, May 1963, 117.

8. "On Being Unchosen by the College of One's Choice," *Saturday Evening Post*, 6 April 1968, 18.

9. "Mothers and Daughters," *New West*, 31 December 1979, 60.

10. *Telling Stories* (Berkeley, Calif.: Bancroft Library, 1978), 4; hereafter cited in the text as *TS*.

11. Iona Opie and Peter Opie, *Oxford Dictionary of Nursery Rhymes* (Oxford: Clarendon, 1951), 65.

12. See Martin Kasindorf, "New Directions for the First Family of Angst," *Saturday Review*, April 1982, 18.

13. Ibid., 15.

14. John Gregory Dunne, *Vegas: A Memoir of a Dark Season* (New York: Warner Books, 1975), 147.

15. "A Problem of Making Connections," *Life*, 5 December 1969, 34.

16. "In Praise of Unhung Wreaths and Love," *Life*, 19 December 1969, 2b (all references are to this page).

17. "Mothers and Daughters," 60.

Chapter Two

1. Review of *Falconer*, by John Cheever. *New York Times Book Review*, 6 March 1977, 1.

2. "Finally (Fashionally) Spurious," *National Review*, 18 November 1961, 342.

3. See *Open Secrets: Ninety-four Women in Touch with Our Time*, ed. Barbaralee Diamonstein (New York: Viking Press, 1970), 104. For a fuller exposition of Didion's views on Elizabeth Hardwick, see her review of Hardwick's *Sleepless Nights* in the *New York Times Book Review*, 29 April 1979, 1, 60.

4. See Sara Davidson, "A Visit with Joan Didion," *New York Times Book Review*, 3 April 1977, 38. On that same page Didion also mentions Conrad, James, and Hemingway as important early influences on her style.

5. "Questions About the New Fiction," *National Review*, 30 November 1965, 1101.

6. For further evidence of Didion's views on Mailer, see her review of Mailer's *An American Dream* in *National Review*, 20 April 1965, 329–30; and of his *The Executioner's Song* in the *New York Times Book Review*, 7 October 1979, 1, 26–27.

7. "Making Up Stories," *Michigan Quarterly Review* 18 (Fall 1979):524.

8. Ibid., 525.

9. Ibid., 528.

10. "Why I Write," *New York Times Book Review*, 5 December 1976, 2.

11. Ibid., 2.

12. There is an even closer similarity between Didion's mode of composition and the one Faulkner employed in writing *The Sound and the Fury*. Speaking of that novel, Faulkner said:

It began with a mental picture. I didn't realize at the time it was symbolical. The picture was of the muddy seat of a little girl's drawers in a pear tree, where she could see through a window where her grandmother's funeral was taking place and report what was happening to her brothers on the ground below. By the time I explained who they were and what they were doing and how her pants got muddy, I realized it would be impossible to get all of it into a short story and that it would have to be a book.

See *Twentieth-Century Interpretations of "The Sound and the Fury,"* ed. Michael H. Cowan (Englewood Cliffs, N.J.: Prentice-Hall, 1968), 16.

13. "Why I Write," 2.

14. Ibid., 98.

15. Ibid., 98.

16. Compare Didion's rendering of the new governor's abode with this description of another California dwelling: the "door was of gumwood painted like fumed oak and it hung on enormous hinges. Although made by machine, the hinges had been carefully stamped to appear hand-forged. The same kind of care and skill had been used to make the roof thatching, which was not really straw but heavy fire-proof paper colored and ribbed to look like straw."

This is not a "real" house but Horace Simpson's bungalow in *The Day of the Locust*, Nathanael West's great surrealistic novel about Southern California. See Nathanael West, *The Complete Works* (New York: Farrar, Straus & Giroux, 1975), 287.

Chapter Three

1. Review of *Falconer*, 1.
2. John Gregory Dunne, *Quintana & Friends* (New York: Dutton, 1978), 254.
3. The title itself comes from the Beatles' "White Album." Released in 1968, this record "was almost the last time the four really worked together, and the fragmentation of the group, the collisions of spirit and explosions in different directions, are apparent in it. 'The White Album' was also a kind of catechism for Manson and his followers. The title of a song from it, 'Helter Skelter,' was written in blood on the refrigerator at the LaBianca House." See Martha Duffy's review of *The White Album* in the *New York Review of Books*, 16 August 1979, 44.
4. *New York Times Book Review*, 17 June 1979, 1.
5. According to Hemingway, "If a writer of prose knows enough about what he is writing about, he may omit things. . . . The dignity of movement of an ice-berg is due to only one-eighth of it being above the water." See *Death in the Afternoon* (New York: Scribner's, 1932), 192.

Chapter Four

1. See Michiko Kakutani, "Joan Didion: Staking Out California," *New York Times Magazine*, 10 June 1979, 40.
2. See Davidson, "A Visit with Jean Didion," 1.
3. Ibid., 36.
4. Susan Braudy, "A Day in the Life of Joan Didion," *Ms.*, February 1977, 66.
5. An uncollected Didion piece that touches on Vietnam is "Fathers, Sons, and Screaming Eagles," *Saturday Evening Post*, 19 October 1968, 27.
6. "On the Last Frontier with VX and GB," *Life*, 20 February 1970, 52 (all references are to this page).
7. In *Bright Book of Life* (Boston: Little, Brown, 1973) Alfred Kazin discusses Didion's work in a chapter on women writers entitled "Cassandras"; it is precisely through the persona of an unheeded prophetess that Didion maintains her ironic perspective on the unexamined optimism of postfrontier Oregon.
8. That was the title of an earlier version of this piece when it appeared in *Life*, 30 January 1970: 20B.

Chapter Five

1. Norman Mailer, *Existential Errands* (Boston: Little, Brown 1972): 3.
2. In the preface of *Slouching Towards Bethlehem* Didion contends that *"writers are always selling somebody out"* (*STB* xiv).
3. See, for example, "I'll Take Romance," *National Review,* 24 September 1963, 248.
4. "Sentimenal Education," *New York Review of Books,* 18 March 1982, 3.
5. Ibid., 6.

Chapter Six

1. Eudora Welty, *The Eye of the Story* (New York: Random House 1978): 128–29.
2. See *The Hymnal of the Protestant Episcopal Church* (New York: Church Hymnal Corporation, 1940), no. 471. Since this hymnal was used during Joan Didion's childhood in the Episcopal Church, it is reasonable to assume that she was familiar with these lines.
3. *Play It as It Lays* (New York: Farrar, Straus & Giroux, 1968), 172; hereafter cited in the text as *PL.*
4. "Getting the Vegas Willies," *Esquire,* May 1977, 44. Although I have chosen not to discuss this essay in detail, it is another example of Didion's ability to evoke a sense of place.

Chapter Seven

1. John Steinbeck, *The Red Pony* (New York: Viking, 1938), 102.
2. Ibid., 119.
3. Kazin, *Bright Book of Life,* 191.
4. "Thinking About Western Thinking," *Esquire,* February 1976, 10.
5. Kazin, *Bright Book of Life,* 190.
6. "Sunset," *Occident,* Spring 1956, 21.
7. Ibid., 23.
8. Ibid., 27.
9. Ibid., 26.
10. "Notes from a Summer Reader," *National Review,* 18 November 1961, 342.
11. *Run River* (New York: Ivan Obolensky, 1963), 210; hereafter cited in the text as *R.*
12. Katherine Usher Henderson argues that the title of Didion's novel comes from the same passage in Ecclesiastes (1:4–7) that served as an epigraph for Hemingway's lost generation novel, *The Sun Also Rises.* See Henderson's *"Run River:* Edenic Vision and Wasteland Nightmare," in *Joan Didion: Essays & Conversations,* ed. Ellen G. Friedman (Princeton, N.J.: Ontario Review Press, 1984), 92.

13. According to this interpretation, Adam and Eve were brother and sister in the Garden, with marriage and childbirth being consequences of the Fall.

14. Linking this scene with the frontier past that is always just beneath the surface of the novel, Jennifer Brady notes that "Lily . . . comes closest to reenacting the role of Tamsen Donner when she holds her dying husband in her arms." See Brady's "Points West, Then and Now: The Fiction of Joan Didion," in *Joan Didion: Essays & Conversations,* 49.

15. In commenting on this scene, Joseph Epstein writes, "*Run River* has something of the feel of Faulkner to it . . . , and very good Faulkner at that" (*Plausible Prejudices,* 247).

16. In addition to the quote from *Peck's 1837 New Guide to the West,* Didion also includes the following epigraph from Robert Lowell's poem "Man and Wife":

> All night I've held your hand,
> as if you had
> a fourth time faced the kingdom of the mad—
> its hackneyed speech, its homicidal eye—
> and dragged me home alive. . . .

Chapter Eight

1. James Joyce, *Dubliners* (New York: Viking, 1961), 210.

2. As Leslie Fiedler has noted, the "Child as Peeping Tom" is something of a stock figure in modern literature. This variation on Freud's primal scene allows the child entrance into the adult world while still remaining technically uncorrupted. See Fiedler's "The Eye of Innocence," in *No! In Thunder: Essays on Myth in Literature* (Boston: Beacon Press, 1960), 280–81.

Chapter Nine

1. The first view can be found in Erica Jong's *How to Save Your Own Life* (New York: Holt, Rinehart & Winston, 1977), 231; the second in Woody Allen's film *Annie Hall.*

2. Dunne, *Quintana & Friends,* 189–90.

3. See "Letter from 'Manhattan,' " *New York Review of Books,* 16 August 1979, 18–19.

4. *Vogue,* 1 January 1964, 24.

5. Cynthia Griffin Wolff goes so far as to see Maria's compulsive freeway driving as a parodic reenactment of frontier rituals ("She drove it as a riverman runs a river, every day more attuned to its currents, its deceptions" [*PL* 16]). See Wolff's "*Play It as It Lays:* Didion and the New American Heroine," in *Joan Didion: Essays & Conversations,* 127.

6. "Why I Write," 98.

7. Guy Davenport, "On the Edge of Being," *National Review*, 25 August 1970, 903.

8. *Bright Book of Life*, 195.

9. Ibid., 195.

10. Such imagery is used even more prominently in the movie version of *Play It as It Lays*. In one particularly memorable scene Maria is watching a television talk show in which Carter is showing and discussing the film *Maria*. Thus we are seeing something that—in terms of Didion's story—purports to be cinema verité but—from our perspective—is actually a film within a TV show within a film.

11. Albert Camus, *The Myth of Sisyphus*, trans. Justin O'Brien (London: Hamish Hamilton, 1955), 11.

12. John Barth, *The Floating Opera*, rev. ed. (Garden City, N.Y.: Doubleday, 1967), 250, 251. Note also the similarity between Todd's reference to Hamlet and Maria's to Iago.

13. In Shaw's *Back to Methuselah* it is the Serpent who says to Eve, "You see things, and you say 'Why?' But I dream things that never were; and I say 'Why not?'" See George Bernard Shaw, *Complete Plays with Prefaces* (New York: Dodd, Mead 1962), 2:7. To compound the irony, at approximately the same time as the events in Didion's novel are supposed to have transpired, Robert Kennedy was adapting this passage from Shaw as a statement of political idealism.

14. "Why I Write," 98.

15. Carlos Baker, *Hemingway: The Writer as Artist* (Princeton: Princeton University Press, 1952), 124.

Chapter Ten

1. *A Book of Common Prayer* (New York: Simon & Schuster, 1977), 13; hereafter cited in the text as *BCP*.

2. For an extended discussion of the Gatsby parallel, see Victor Strandberg, "Passion and Delusion in *A Book of Common Prayer*," in *Joan Didion: Essays & Conversations*, 147–63.

3. In this regard he resembles John McClellan, for whom "Easterners fell into two camps: goddamn pansies and goddamn Jews" (*R* 57).

4. Robert Scholes and Robert Kellogg, *The Nature of Narrative* (New York: Oxford University Press, 1966), 261.

5. Ibid., 261–62.

6. See Davidson, "A Visit with Joan Didion," 36.

7. Ibid., 37.

8. See ibid., 38.

Chapter Eleven

1. See George F. Will, "Didion's Book Fluent in 'Caring.' " Syndicated column distributed by the *Washington Post* Writers Group the week of 20 May 1984.

2. Gene Lyons, "Slouching Through Salvador," *Newsweek*, 28 March 1983, 69.

3. *Salvador* (New York: Simon & Schuster, 1983), 17; hereafter cited in the text as *S*.

4. Dunne, *Quintana & Friends*, 174.

5. There are a couple of places in this book where Didion admits that the story she is dealing with may not lend itself to her repertoire of standard rhetorical devices. At one point she finds an irony that almost begs to be exploited and says, "I realized that I was no longer much interested in this kind of irony, that this was a story that would not be illuminated by such details" (*S* 36). Later, in reference to another "literary" discovery, she says, "it occurred to me that this was the first time in my life that I had been in the presence of obvious 'material' and felt no professional exhilaration at all, only personal dread" (*S* 56).

6. See James Atlas, "Slouching Towards Miami," *Vanity Fair*, October 1987, 52.

7. *Miami* (New York: Simon & Schuster, 1987), 83; hereafter cited in the text as *M*.

Chapter Twelve

1. See "Honolulu Days," *New West*, 14 July 1980, 25–27.

2. "Where *Tonight Show* Guests Go to Rest," *Esquire*, October 1976, 25.

3. See Will, "Didion's Book Fluent in 'Caring.' "

4. Mary McCarthy, "Love and Death in the Pacific," *New York Times Book Review*, 22 April 1984, 19.

5. *Democracy* (New York: Simon & Schuster, 1984), 104; hereafter cited in the text as *D*.

6. Ibid., 19. For Didion's personal observations about the situation in Kuala Lampur, see "Boat People," *New West*, 25 February, 1980, 59–60.

7. Thomas R. Edwards, "An American Education," *New York Review of Books*, 10 May 1984, 24.

8. "Nuclear Blue," *New West*, 5 November 1979, 77–78.

9. Thomas Mallon, review of *Democracy, American Spectator*, August 1984, 44.

10. In the German sections of *Vanity Fair* Thackeray speaks of having met Amelia and Dobbin; in *Adam Bede* Eliot treats her characters as if they

were historical persons and introduces herself into the story when discussing the respective merits of parsons Irwine and Ryde.

11. The Tropical Belt Coal Company can be found in Conrad's *Nostromo*. I have no idea where the "leper at the door" comes from, but I suspect that the "lone figure on the crest of the immutable hill" is an allusion to Edwin Arlington Robinson's "Man Against the Sky."

Chapter Thirteen

1. Mark Schorer, "Novels and Nothingness," *American Scholar*, 40 (Winter 1970–71):174.

2. D. A. N. Jones, "Divided Selves," *New York Review of Books*, 22 October 1970, 42.

Selected Bibliography

PRIMARY SOURCES

Fiction

A Book of Common Prayer. New York: Simon and Schuster, 1977.
Democracy. New York: Simon & Schuster, 1984.
Play It as It Lays. New York: Farrar, Straus & Giroux, 1968.
Run River. New York: Ivan Obolensky, 1963.
Telling Stories. Berkeley: Bancroft Library, 1978.

Nonfiction

Miami. New York: Simon & Schuster, 1987.
Salvador. New York: Simon & Schuster, 1983.
Slouching Towards Bethlehem. New York: Farrar, Straus & Giroux, 1968.
The White Album. New York: Simon & Schuster, 1979.

Uncollected Prose (since 1979)

For a relatively complete and reasonably accurate listing of Joan Didion's
uncollected prose through October 1979, see Donna Olendorf below.
"Boat People." *New West*, 25 February 1980, 59–60.
"Discovery." Review of *Finding the Center: Two Narratives*, by V. S. Naipaul,
and *Getting to Know the General*, by Graham Greene. *New York Review of
Books*, 11 October 1984, 10, 12.
"Honolulu Days." *New West*, 14 July 1980, 25–27.
"Mothers and Daughters." *New West*, 31 December 1979, 59–60.
"The Need to Know." *New West*, 5 May 1980, 86, 88.
"Nuclear Blue." *New West*, 5 November 1979, 77–78.
"Sentimental Education." Review of *Every Secret Thing*, by Patricia Campbell
Hearst with Alvin Moscow. *New York Review of Books*, 18 March 1982,
3–4, 6.
"Without Regret or Hope." Review of *The Return of Eva Peron with the Killings
in Trinidad*, by V. S. Naipaul. *New York Review of Books*, 12 June 1980,
20–21.

SECONDARY SOURCES

Bibliography

Jacobs, Fred Rue. *Joan Didion—Bibliography.* Keene, California: Loop Press,
  1977. A useful, though flawed, bibliography of both primary and secondary sources. Contains numerous printing errors—particularly within its
  listing of secondary material.
Olendorf, Donna. "Joan Didion: A Checklist, 1955–1980," *Bulletin of Bibliography* 32 (January–March 1981):32–44. The most thorough and accurate bibliography of both primary and secondary material now available.

Biography and General Criticism

Brady, Jennifer. "Points West, Then and Now: The Fiction of Joan Didion."
  Contemporary Literature 20 (1979):452–70. Reprinted in Friedman, 44–
  59. An application of the Turner thesis to *Run River, Play It as It Lays, A
  Book of Common Prayer,* and "When Did Music Come This Way?"
Braudy, Susan. "A Day in the Life of Joan Didion," *Ms.,* February 1977, 65–
  68, 108–9. An account of an interview with Didion, complete with Ms.
  Braudy's own feminist commentary.
Coale, Samuel, "Didion's Disorder: An American Romancer's Art." *Critique:
  Studies in Modern Fiction* 25, no. 1 (1984):160–70. A discussion of Did-
  ion's first three novels. "American myths haunt Didion as they did
  Hawthorne. His cold eye cast upon transcendental aspirations and Emer-
  sonian new selves becomes her version of America's mystic West."
Davidson, Sara. "A Visit with Joan Didion." *New York Times Book Review,* 3
  April 1977, 1, 35–38. Reprinted in Friedman, 13–21. An excellent
  interview with Didion shortly after the publication of *A Book of Common
  Prayer.*
Diamonstein, Barbaralee. *Open Secrets: Ninety-four Women in Touch with Our
  Time.* New York: Viking Press, 1970, 103–6. Didion is one of ninety-
  four women to respond briefly to some general and rather superficial
  questions.
Dunne, John Gregory. *Quintana & Friends.* New York: Dutton, 1978. Col-
  lection of essays sheds light on the home life of the Dunnes.
————. *Vegas: A Memoir of a Dark Season.* 1974. Rpt. New York: Warner
  Books, 1975. An autobiographical narrative about a difficult time in the
  marriage of Didion and Dunne.
Epstein, Joseph. "The Sunshine Girls: Renata Adler and Joan Didion." *Plausible Prejudices.* New York: Norton, 1985, 238–53. "There is a plain
  pessimism and there is heroic pessimism—and of plain pessimism, of the

kind Renata Adler and Joan Didion dispense, we have had quite enough."

Friedman, Ellen G., editor. *Joan Didion: Essays and Conversations.* Princeton, N.J.: Ontario Review Press, 1984. Contains Didion's "Why I Write," three "conversations" with the author, and fourteen essays by various hands.

Henderson, Katherine Usher. *Joan Didion.* New York: Ungar, 1981. A brief but helpful introductory study.

Kakutani, Michiko. "Joan Didion: Staking Out California." *New York Times Magazine,* 10 June 1979, 34, 36, 38, 40, 44, 46, 48, 50. Reprinted in Friedman, 29–40. An informative biographical feature that appeared just prior to the publication of *The White Album.*

Kasindorf, Martin. "New Directions for the First Family of Angst." *Saturday Review,* April 1982, 14–18. A feature article on Didion and Dunne written to coincide with the publication of *Dutch Shea Jr.*

Kazin, Alfred. *Bright Book of Life: American Novelists and Storytellers from Hemingway to Mailer.* Boston: Little, Brown, 1973, 189–98. A short critical account of Didion's career through *Play It as It Lays.*

———. "Joan Didion: Portrait of a Professional." *Harper's,* December 1971, 112–14, 116, 118, 120–22. Biographical and critical essay, part of which later appeared in *Bright Book of Life.*

Lahr, John. "Entrepreneurs of Anxiety." *Horizon,* January 1981, 36, 38–39. A vitriolic attack on Didion and Dunne as "brilliant mirrors of the California bourgeoise."

Mallon, Thomas. "The Limits of History in the Novels of Joan Didion." *Critique: Studies in Modern Fiction* 21, no. 3 (1980):43–52. Reprinted in Friedman, 60–67. A discussion of Didion's first three novels. "All of Didion's heroines have trouble with history, personal and otherwise, and each of her novels is an attempt at travelling backwards in search of various historical explanations."

Newton, Judith. "Joan Didion, 1972." *Female Studies VI: Closer to the Ground.* Edited by Nancy Hoffman, Cynthia Secor, and Adrian Tinsley. Old Westbury, N.Y.: Feminist Press, 1972, 110–15. An attempt to demonstrate inconsistencies between the political attitudes expressed in "The Women's Movement" and Didion's own literary practice.

Stimpson, Catherine. "The Case of Miss Joan Didion." *Ms.,* January 1973, 36–41. Feminist attack on Didion as "a curious creature, whose sense of literature and life is common, disappointingly conventional, and always problematical."

Winchell, Mark Royden. *John Gregory Dunne.* Boise: Boise State University Western Writers Series, 1986. An overview of the career of Joan Didion's husband through 1984.

On Specific Works

A Book of Common Prayer

Hollowell, John. "Against Interpretation: Narrative Strategy in *A Book of Common Prayer.*" In Friedman, 164–76. A deconstructionist reading of *A Book of Common Prayer.*

Merivale, Patricia. "Through Greeneland in Drag: Joan Didion's *A Book of Common Prayer.*" *Pacific Coast Philology* 15 (1980):45–52. A comparison of *A Book of Common Prayer* with Graham Greene's *The Quiet American.* Stresses the theme of female bonding within the context of the elegiac romance.

Oates, Joyce Carol. "A Taut Novel of Disorder." Review of *A Book of Common Prayer. New York Times Book Review,* 3 April 1977, 1, 34–35. Reprinted in Friedman, 138–41. Didion has been an articulate witness to the most stubborn and intractable truths of our time, a memorable voice . . . , always in control."

Raphael, Frederick. "Grace Under Pressure." Review of *A Book of Common Prayer. Saturday Review,* 5 March 1977: 23–25. One senses in Didion "the quick desire for something more noble, more tender, and more enduring than crass contemporary 'realism.' "

Romano, John. "Joan Didion and Her Characters." Review of *A Book of Common Prayer. Commentary,* July 1977, 61–63. Reprinted in Friedman, 142–46. Sees Grace's story as "an allegory of the progress of the liberal, humanisitic intelligence in the last twenty years."

Strandberg, Victor. "Passion and Delusion in *A Book of Common Prayer.*" *Modern Fiction Studies* 27, no. 2 (1981):225–42. Reprinted in Friedman, 147–63. A brilliant analysis of *A Book of Common Prayer* as "a female counterpart to *The Great Gatsby.*"

Democracy

Edwards, Thomas R. "An American Education." Review of *Democracy. New York Review of Books,* 10 May 1984, 23–24. "*Democracy* is absorbing, immensely intelligent, and witty, and it finally earns its complexity of form."

Hitchens, Christopher. "The Lovett Latitudes." Review of *Democracy. Times Literary Supplement,* 14 September 1984, 1018. "The staccato organization and the style of the novel make it both easy and difficult to read. One is reminded of the rapid cross-cutting that Hollywood . . . has imposed on modern narrative."

McCarthy, Mary. "Love and Death in the Pacific." Review of *Democracy. New York Times Book Review,* 22 April 1984, 1, 18–19. "The construction of 'Democracy' feels like the working out of a jigsaw puzzle that is slowly being put together with a continual shuffling and reexamination of pieces still on the edges or heaped in the middle of the design."

Mallon, Thomas. Review of *Democracy. American Spectator,* August 1984, 43–44. "I have not been so disappointed by a novel in years—partly because as *Democracy* clanks along Didion keeps giving brief reminders of her exquisite gifts."

Tyler, Anne. "Affairs of State." Review of *Democracy. New Republic,* 9 April 1984, 35–36. "[I]t may be that the reader's journey here is not toward a happy ending, or even an unhappy ending, but toward adopting the narrator's vision of the world."

Will, George F. "Didion's Book Fluent in 'Caring.' " Syndicated column distributed by *Washington Post* Writers Group the week of 20 May 1984. "Some readers may decide that Didion's novel is less about politics than it is about the manners and cost of celebrity. Didion suggests that the latter subject is now a large facet of the former."

Miami

Atlas, James. "Slouching Towards Miami." *Vanity Fair,* October 1987, 48, 52, 56. A conversation with Didion prior to the publication of *Miami.* "The world she once perceived as out of control, a world of violence and random murder, has come to possess a king of logic."

Chace, James. "Betrayals and Obsessions." Review of *Miami. New York Times Book Review,* 25 October 1987, 3. "The world Miss Didion describes in beautifully evocative prose is that familiar landscape we have come to expect from her novels and essays."

Cohen, Jeffrey C. "Metaphor for the Future." Review of *Miami* and two other books on the city. *National Review,* 20 November 1987, 54, 56–58. "A thoroughly muddled picture, a swarm of insinuated accusations, and precious little enlightenment."

Wilson, Robert. "Books." *USA Today,* 16 December 1987, 4D. Lists *Miami* among the worst nonfiction books of 1987. "At least her *Salvador* suggests that she went there; this reads like notes from *The Miami Herald.*"

Play It as It Lays

Chabot, C. Barry. "Joan Didion's *Play It as It Lays* and the Vacuity of the Here and Now." *Critique: Studies in Modern Fiction* 21, no. 3 (1980):53–60. Reprinted in Friedman, 117–23. Sees Maria as a willing victim. "[T]he passivity of sanitarium life represents for her a haven from the world that appears to offer only causes for grievance."

Geherin, David J. "Nothingness and Beyond: Joan Didion's *Play It as It Lays.*" *Critique: Studies in Modern Fiction* 16, no. 1 (1974):64–78. Reprinted in Friedman, 105–116. Discusses novel within the context of Camus's philosophy. Sees Maria as having "pushed beyond nothingness to a limited affirmation of meaning."

Jones, D. A. N. "Divided Selves." Review of *Play It as It Lays. New York*

Review of Books, 22 October 1970, 38–42. Finds in the novel "a certain exhilaration, as when we appreciate a harmonious and well-proportioned painting of some cruelly martyred saint in whom we do not believe."

Leonard, John. "The Cities of the Desert, the Desert of the Mind." *New York Times*, 21 July 1970, 33. "There hasn't been another American writer of Joan Didion's quality since Nathanael West. . . . [Her vision in *Play It as It Lays*] is as bleak and precise as Eliot's in *The Waste Land*."

Schorer, Mark. "Novels and Nothingness." Review of *Play It as It Lays*. *American Scholar* 40 (Winter 1970–71):169, 170, 172, 174. When reading this novel "one thinks of the great *performers* in ballet, opera, circuses." It is "a triumph not of insight as such but of style."

Wolff, Cynthia Griffin. "*Play It as It Lays:* Didion and the New American Heroine." In Friedman, 124–37. Sees *Play It as It Lays* as an examination of the (patriarchal) legacy of American puritanism.

Run River

Davenport, Guy. "Midas' Grandchildren." Review of *Run River*. *National Review*, 7 May 1963, 371. Dialogue between an imaginary "critic" and "reader." Makes good interpretive points about the novel, but is perplexing in its point of view.

Henderson, Katherine U. "*Run River:* Edenic Vision and Wasteland Nightmare." In Friedman, 91–104. A suggestive attempt to read *Run River* at both an historic and mythic level.

"Lily of the Valley." Review of *Run River*. *Times Literary Supplement*, 30 January 1964, 92. Calls *Run River* "a beautifully told first novel." "Written in prose both witty and imaginative, it has too a high level of intelligence."

Mauer, Robert. "Lifeless by the Fruitful Sacramento." Review of *Run River*. *New York Herald Tribune Book Review*, 12 May 1963, 10. Argues that, despite her technical proficiency, Didion—unlike Philip Roth—does not see life "as possessing a tang."

Salvador

Eder, George Jackson. "The Little World of Joan Didion." Review of *Salvador*. *National Review*, 8 July 1983, 829–30. "Those who seek the facts behind the Salvadoran situation would do better to listen to the reasoned views of Dr. Jeanne Jordan Kirkpatrick than to the more strident tones of Mrs. Joan Didion Dunne."

Falcoff, Mark. "Two Weeks." Review of *Salvador*. *Commentary*, May 1983, 66, 68–70. Didion "makes the tiny republic of El Salvador into a mirror reflecting her own basic contempt for liberal democracy and . . . the American way of life."

Hanley, Lynne T. "To El Salvador." *Massachusetts Review* 24, no. 1 (1983):13–

29. A discussion of Didion's treatment of war in *A Book of Common Prayer* and *Salvador.*

Hoge, Warren. "A Land Without Solid Ground." Review of *Salvador. New York Times Book Review,* 13 March 1983, 3, 30. "No one in El Salvador has interpreted the place better. . . . Her novelist's eye examines policy on a plane seldom reached in Congressional hearings or State Department briefings."

Kiley, Frederick. "Beyond Words: Narrative Art in Joan Didion's *Salvador.*" In Friedman, 181–88. "Didion sees the modern guise of evil in this hideous landscape . . . , revealing the awful capacities that lie dormant in the human heart of darkness."

Lyons, Gene. "Slouching Through Salvador." Review of *Salvador. Newsweek,* 28 March 1983, 69. "Most readers will not get very far in this very short book without wondering whether she visited that sad and tortured place less to report than to validate the Didion world view."

Slouching Towards Bethlehem

Johnson, Michael. *The New Journalism.* Lawrence: University of Kansas Press, 1971, 96–100. Compares *Slouching Towards Bethlehem* with the writings of Truman Capote, Tom Wolfe, and Dan Wakefield.

"Somewhere Else." Review of *Slouching Towards Bethlehem. Times Literary Supplement,* 12 February 1970, 153. "Between her provincial roots and the two cosmopolitan coasts, between her Happy Valley and urban paranoia, Joan Didion wanders, slightly dazed but acutely observant."

Wakefield, Dan. Review of *Slouching Towards Bethlehem. New York Times Book Review,* 21 July 1968, 8. *Slouching* is "a rich display of some of the best prose written in this country."

The White Album

Duffy, Martha. "Pictures from an Expedition." Review of *The White Album. New York Review of Books,* 16 August 1979, 43–44. "The essays in *The White Album* . . . in some ways . . . are better than her fiction, because in her novels she submerges her own voice."

Malin, Irving. "The Album of Anxiety." In Friedman, 177–80. A facile summary of the title essay of *The White Album.*

Simon, John. "De Tenuissimis Clamavi." Review of *The White Album. National Review,* 12 October 1979, 1311–12. "After reading such outpourings of hypersensitivity in quotidian conflict, one feels positively relieved to be an insensitive clod."

Towers, Robert. "The Decline and Fall of the 60's." Review of *The White Album. New York Times Book Review,* 17 June 1979, 1, 30. Didion's "is a voice like no other in comtemporary journalism."

Index